Contents

The 50 Greatest Beers
in the World

The 50 Greatest Beers in the World

AN EXPERT'S RANKING
OF THE VERY BEST

STUART A. KALLEN

A CITADEL PRESS BOOK
Published by Carol Publishing Group

A Citadel Press Book
Published by Carol Publishing Group
Citadel Press is a registered trademark of Carol Communications, Inc.

Editorial, sales and distribution, rights and permissions inquiries should be addressed to Carol Publishing Group, 120 Enterprise Avenue, Secaucus, N.J. 07094

In Canada: Canadian Manda Group, One Atlantic Avenue, Suite 105, Toronto, Ontario, M6K 3E7

Carol Publishing Group Books may be purchased in bulk at special discounts for sales promotion, fund-raising, or educational purposes. Special editions can be created to specifications. For details, contact Special Sales Department, 120 Enterprise Avenue, Secaucus, N.J. 07094.

Book design by Robert Freese

MANUFACTURED IN THE UNITED STATES OF AMERICA

10 9 8 7 6 5 4 3 2 1

LIBRARY OF CONGRESS CATALOGING-IN-PUBLICATION DATA

Kallen, Stuart A., 1955–
    The 50 greatest beers in the world : an expert's ranking of the very best / Stuart A. Kallen.
        p.   cm.
    "A Citadel Press book."
    Includes bibliographical references.
    ISBN 0–8065–1841–3 (pb)
    1. Beer.   I. Title
TP577.K35   1996
641.2'3—dc20   96–30963
                                                               CIP

Preface

Cerevisia malorum . . . divina medicina
(A little bit of beer is divine medicine)
—PARACELSUS, 16TH-CENTURY PHYSICIAN

I drank a thousand different beers to get where I am today. Not many people can make that claim. I could make it but it wouldn't be true. The actual number is closer to two thousand, give or take a few.

But there's just *something* about a great beer that gets my attention. You can taste ten pale ales in a row—and I have—but only one (or maybe two) is going to be memorable. Make no mistake, a very few select beers are better than all the others. And there are reasons why that is so. The brewers of great beers know that it takes time, serious human effort, technical skills, and only the finest ingredients to make a great beer. They are uncompromising in their intentions and armed with the expertise of their ancient ancestors.

Why should anyone care about great beer? Because there are rare and beautiful things in superlative beer that cannot be found anywhere else. To wit:

- Great beers relieve us of life's stresses and strains in ways that have been medically proven as healthful.
- Fine beer is inspirational. It has kindled the creative fires of many a poet, artist, and musician.
- Good beer is a social lubricant that allows us to enjoy conversation with strangers and near strangers.
- A quality beer will help us forget the troubles and negative energies of the day.
- Great beer fills our bellies with hop herb and malt energy.

I ask you: What's not to like?

I learned a great deal writing this book. Beer has an ancient lineage. Reading beer history, I sometimes wonder if evolution is nothing more than yeast coercing humans to do their bidding.

And you'll be glad to know I'm not the only one who thinks the beers in this book are the world's best. Many of the beers herein have won officially sanctioned gold, silver, platinum, and bronze medals for their quality and, dare I say, artistry.

I don't work for any beer company. No one has asked me to sing the praises of the beers in this book. Maybe some wouldn't want me to. But in general, this world is filled with schlock. Every little thing has been incorporated, encrusted in plastic, mass marketed, oversold, product placed, focus grouped, and groped. This includes all of the major food groups—including love and sex! After watching the Nth-billionth commercial for weak, pissy, mass-produced suds and seeing the tank drainings of some hundred-acre brewing complex sold as "handcrafted beer," it's nice to know that there are still millions of us who won't take schlock for an answer.

Welcome to the club.

In this day and age there are absolutely zero reasons to go along with the crowd when it comes to our finest possession—taste. As Shakespeare didn't say: "Life's too short to drink bad beer."

My guess is that, if asked, nine out of ten doctors would recommend that *if you're going to drink beer, you should drink only the best.* Just like the scientifically proven life-enhancing qualities of red wine, great beers contain unique chemical compounds that can be found only in that specific product. A beer produced in a brewery that is over 425 years old, for example, would have medicinal values, vitamins, and mineral compounds contained in the unique strains of yeasts that could be found nowhere else on earth. Who knows what natural genetic mutations that yeast has undergone to bring us the finest flavors in all history? The same rings true with strains of malt and hops.

I drank a hell of a lot of beer to write this book. I felt it was my duty. Laugh, but I wanted to be sure that the beers I am recommending are only the best. I'm an easily bored person. But I was never bored by the beer listed here, because each beer has its own character. Of course I tasted only the best 250 beers in the world before I felt sure. I had to draw the line somewhere.

What I ask of anybody who drinks beer is this: You don't eat fruit unless it's fresh. You don't buy USDA Grade B steaks. Why, oh why, would you drink anything but the finest-quality handcrafted beer? There *is* a difference.

It comes down to intent. What was the *intention* of the brewery that produced the beer? Many European breweries have an almost religious reverence for the beer they produce; so do American and Canadian micro-brewers. But what's the intent of Budoors or Swiller Brewing? I don't personally believe that they have my best interests in mind, or they wouldn't try to sell me swill.

A great beer can satisfy every basic primal human need: It's wet. It's refreshing. It seems that—at least temporarily—nothing, anywhere is as good, as perfect, or as ambrosial as that moment when it meets your lips. The place you are standing becomes irrelevant. You're taken to a time and place where the piquancy in the back of your throat tastes of an innate understanding of existence that is timeless. Whew!

Great beer is infinite. It transcends time and space. It takes you to a locale and epoch in history. When the Westphalia brewery in Germany says that it is the oldest brewery in the world, that's no idle boast. Can you name me a bakery that's 550 years old? How about a department store? A government?

Almost nothing has lasted longer in history as an intact product than beer. Breweries whose product we may sample every day are using yeast strains from the time of Michelangelo.

Great beers contain a long memory. Think of beer as bottled air. Because it is a bottle full of carbon dioxide. Think of beer as bottled water. Of that there is no doubt. Think of beer as food. Most people in the world do. Beer is sustenance—mental and physical—in a world full of uncertainty. What's the best beer? I hope I can help you decide.

I invite you to purchase some of the beers in this book, turn off the TV, put down the newspaper, take the phone off the hook, put on some tunes, and enjoy them with me. It is my honor to explain the details and history of the beers for your edification.

Here's to good taste and all the finer things in life. Cheers!

Acknowledgments

First and foremost I'd like to dedicate this to my sweetheart, Patti Marlene Boekhoff, without whose wise observations and infinite patience this book would not have been beer-able.

A heartfelt thanks to my good friends Shari Moore and Jonathan Chaplain, Barb and Pam Dorset, and Abra and Chris Coleman-Weber for providing inspiration and sustenance throughout.

I'd like to thank Jim Ellison and the folks at Citadel Press for having the wisdom and foresight to call me to write this book.

A big thank-you to those folks in the beer business who work day and night to insure all of us an unending supply of great beer! It's a labor of love, and I wish continued success to Peter Brey at Heineken USA, William Lynch at Guinness Import, Wendy Littlefield and Don Feinberg at Vanberg and Dewulf, Ben Myers at Hart Brewing, Cathy Noah at Rogue, George Saxon at Phoenix Imports, Matthias and Stephanie Neidhart at B. United International, Charles Finkel and Lynn Kastner at Merchant du Vin, Lanny at All Saint's Brands, and the folks at Oasis and Anderson Valley Brewing, to name but a few.

The Scribes of Beer (S.O.B.s) also deserve my gratitude: Bill Owens at *BeeR: the magazine* and *American Brewer*; Sara and Phil Doersam at *Southern Draft*; and Bill Metzger and Joe Barfield at *Southwest Brewing News*.

Here's to all the hardworking folks who play the coppers and tuns at the breweries like fine instruments and bust their butts to bring us all some of life's best.

And to Heather Nova and Enya for their inspirational music that magically sustained me through Ireland as well as through many a long day at my computer.

To everyone—skoal!

Introduction

When I was first asked by my editor to rate the beers in this book I was slightly skeptical. It's tough comparing a German weizenbock to an English pale ale to an American pilsner. But when I threw myself into the task, I realized that I was having fun. And with the agreement of my self-ensconced panel of experts I could actually sense one beer being slightly more enjoyable than the next. And when I say slightly, I mean incremental amounts of joy.

There is very little difference in quality between the number one beer in this book and number fifty, whereas you could drive a truck through the difference between the fifty beers in this book and ninety percent of the mass-produced beers in your favorite bottle shop. After much soul searching, returning to the beers again and again, and general research, I feel that I made the right choices.

Most of the tasting was done blind—and I don't mean blind drunk. I sat down with five or six beers of a particular style and drank small amounts of them while rating my impressions, much in the same way as home-brewing contests are judged.

A little background: I've been in beer tastings with the so-called world experts. I've judged home-brew contests, I've hung out with brewers, and I'm a home brewer myself.

I used many criteria to reach my conclusions, and rating each beer was one of the most difficult things I've ever done in my life. I tried to avoid politics, but every brewer thinks his or her beer is the best. I hope I didn't offend anyone by putting one beer before another. I value my friendships, old and new, in the beer business and hope everyone understands that their beer wouldn't be in this book if it wasn't better than the other twenty-five hundred commonly available beers. I tried to be as merciless as possible and still take into account many things that can affect the taste of even the greatest beer.

I can comfortably claim that the beers listed in this book are the best there are. Quality, tradition, and impeccable attention to detail are not just advertising slogans. I'd like to personally thank the brewers and importers who work day and night to make sure that I can walk into a bottle shop in my town and be mystically transported on a magic carpet of malt, hops, and yeast to a better time and space.

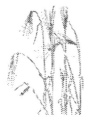

PART ONE

And the
Winner Is . . .

1

What Makes a Beer Great?

You may think it's easy spending time tasting—really tasting—hundreds of different beers. And I must admit, I can't complain (though sometimes I still do). The hardest part about writing this book was not "What is the best beer?" but "How can I pick only fifty among so many?" This task would have been immeasurably easier even three years ago. But with the explosive growth of the microbrewing industry, some brewers have enough experience under their belts by now to rival the great brewers of Europe. Hell, some of them *are* the great brewers of Europe who now make the United States their home. And new beers are put on the market literally every week.

When people ask me, "What *is* the best beer?" I always tell them, "Your locally produced microbrewed beer." It may not always be true, but fresh beer is usually the best beer. Now if your local brewpub has been in business for six months, they're obviously not going to rival the quality of a five-hundred-year-old brewery in Germany. But nine times out of ten, you'll get a beer that's been lovingly crafted and handled minimally. That can make all the difference. Besides, it's up to each and every one of us to support our local craft brewery. If they're still making beer in the year 2397, they'll have you to thank.

That said, a truly great beer should take you away to a different time and place. The Trappist beers of Belgium smell, taste, and feel like the mystical, meditative, and ancient tradition embodied by the Benedictine Brothers who brew them. They can and should be drunk with reverence.

Yeast has a genetic memory. Some of the yeast strains used by European brewers are directly related to yeasts that have lived during the Renaissance—maybe in Babylonian antiquity. So too with hops and barley. Tiny patches of farm fields scattered across Europe have been growing the same strain of barleycorn in the same place for hundreds of years. This gives the beers made with these ancient ingredients a consistent quality that is practically immovable. Napoleon couldn't stop them, and neither could two world wars. That's a genetic memory.

So when we partake of a great beer, we too are touching something in our genetic memories—and it may also be in our present memory. Does the beer taste like a waving field of wheat? Does it smell like the salty Pacific high tide? Fresh Muenster cheese? Alder-smoked salmon? Does it remind you of the sparkle of the Alpine sky or a lonesome barley field in North Dakota? That's a tough criteria for judging a beer. But after tasting thousands of beers, I have found that some do live up to the challenge.

A great beer should have its own personality. Upon first sip it should announce that you are dealing with a contender. A true contender will last and last all the way down to the bottom of the glass. A truly great beer will have you wringing the final drop from the bottle. You might not like a beer's personality—say a smoky doppelbock—but you will still know that the personality is there. No way would it be confused with a mass-produced American pilsner.

A great beer should inspire one to poetry, to song, to love, to romance. How can that be bottled? Maybe it's the memory of the magic of ancient Egypt. Maybe it's generations of loving knowledge that have been applied to the beer's production. Maybe you're drunk.

Yes, beer can make one drunk. But with fine beer, it's a different sort of euphoria. There's a calmness and purpose of spirit present—flashes of bottled brilliance—and discretion to warn one away from overindulgence. And if one should drink with too much gusto, great beers can be a little more forgiving. Bottle-conditioned beers (those bottled with live yeast) contain B vitamins—a proven hangover preventative.

A lot has been made of the Reinheitsgebot, the sixteenth-century Bavarian beer-purity law that states beer should be made only from malted barley, hops, and water. (And wheat beers from wheat; yeast had not yet been isolated and named.) It is true that most of the great beers of the world follow the Reinheitsgebot, but there's plenty of swill that contains only those basic ingredients. Conversely, some of the best beers in the world—most notably Belgian and English—use various candy sugars to give their beers fascinating and unique tastes. Some beers also contain fruit (such as peaches and raspberries) and spices (from cardamom to juniper). So while the Reinheitsgebot is a good rule of thumb when shopping for a beer, it isn't the be-all and end-all of quality beers.

The main destroyer of good beer is shipping and handling. Beer is volatile. When it's rocking across oceans and continents in a train, plane, or truck, it's like Elvis—all shook up—by the time it reaches your refrigerator. Remarkably, ninety-five percent of the time, it's in good, drinkable shape. But there's no guarantee that a beer your drinking, from five, fifty, or five thousand miles away, has survived the journey. I've had two different beers from the same six-pack wherein one was good, the other bad.

Nowadays more and more breweries are freshness-dating their beers on the label. This gives the drinker an accurate picture of the beer's age. Unless the beer is a high-alcohol offering, it's usually best when drunk before three months in the bottle—at most, six months. The greatest beer in the world might be sitting on the shelf in your local bottle shop. But if no one buys it, it's not going to last forever. Sigh. Such a waste.

Any particular draft beer is almost always better than its bottled counterpart. The best beer in the world can be turned to trash by the simple act of putting it in a bottle. Brewing beer is one thing. Bottling beer is a whole 'nother animal. They are two different and distinct acts that some brewers—especially newer microbreweries—are still learning to grapple with. If you take said bottled beer, load it on a train, and rattle it off to East Cockleburr, then you are really pushing your flavor physics around. Shaking beer for hours at a time is not the way to improve it.

The European brewers have an edge here. After all, they were shipping beer halfway around the world in barrels before Paul Revere's horse was born. They did it in wood barrels; they did it in ceramic bottles; they did it in glass. The English even brewed it aboard ships on the open ocean during both world wars. Of course the Egyptians traded it around before Tut was a teenager.

I have had to stick primarily to bottled beer for the purposes of this book. Unfortunately, I don't know of a pub in North America that has every beer in this book on tap. (If one exists, someone please tell me where it is. I want to move next door.) Many of the world's great bottled beers are bottle conditioned and are therefore still "working" and still "alive" while being shipped. For this reason, bottle-conditioned beers survive travel much better than those that have been pasteurized, which kills the living yeast in the beer.

Again I will reiterate: If you can sit in a taproom adjoining a brewery, you're probably getting the best right there. But variety is the spice of life—even if it's in a bottle from six thousand miles away.

2

You Is What You Taste

Before we get into the actual beer ratings, I'd like to give a refresher course on the science of the tongue and tasting so you can get a feel for how I arrived at some of my conclusions. Research! Research! Research!

As you know, good beer is made of four basic ingredients—malted barley, hops, yeast, and water. Wheat, fruit, candy sugar, and spices are sometimes—but usually not—added. The main four ingredients can be combined into thousands of subtle flavors, smells, and nuances.

Just as beer has four basic ingredients, your tongue is designed to pick up four basic flavors—sweet, sour, salty, and bitter. Those four receptors can determine something like thirty thousand different flavors.

In primal terms, the sweet taste buds determine which foods might be nutritious and worthy of eating. The salty buds tell you that certain foods might replace the vital minerals lost to sweat and other bodily fluids. The sour buds warn you away from foods that might make you sick. And the bitter buds set off the mental alarms cautioning you that a substance you're about to eat might be poisonous. But it's obviously not that simple.

That pink little muscle flapping around in your mouth is much more complicated than it looks in the mirror. The little protruding dots on your tongue are called papillae, and there are four different kinds of papillae. Each one contains from 2 to 250 taste buds. There are two kinds of taste buds—receptor and basal. When you taste something, there are chemical reactions with your saliva that send molecules into the taste buds. Taste buds communicate with each other and decide what signal to send to your brain. If you're lucky they say "good beer." If you're not, they might say "bad oysters." Luckily, we don't have to think about our taste buds. It all happens in a split second.

You might remember from your high school biology class the map of the tongue that showed the sweet-detecting buds on the tip of the tongue and the salt-detecting buds on each side. The sour buds were shown on the back-sides of the tongue, and the last defense against gag-a-licious foods were the bitter buds at the back of the tongue. If you think that sounds too orderly for nature, you're right. All taste buds are capable of detecting all flavors, although some that are more sensitive to certain flavors are clustered in the aforementioned places. You even have taste buds in your upper palate.

All of this info would be irrelevant if it weren't for the nose. Everyone who's had a cold knows that with a plugged nose you could be eating an apple or a rutabaga for all your tongue can tell. When you eat, the vapors of the food travel up your nose before they ever come in contact with the tongue. When you chew, the vapors go up the back of your throat to your nasal cavities. There, molecules of flavor hit postage-stamp-sized tissue called the olfactory membrane. Every nasal cavity has one, and each one contains one hundred million receptor cells. Through complicated and miraculous chemical reaction, those billions of cells tell more billions of cells to send more signals to different parts of your brain. Some signals go to the hypothalamus, which controls such primitive feelings as appetite, anger, fear, and pleasure. Other signals go to your memory-regulating brain. Some go deeper into your subconscious.

That's why odors can provoke such powerful emotions. And that's what a great beer can also accomplish. The smell, taste, and feel can evoke ancient Sumeria, the salty North Sea, sunny France, or any other of hundreds of pictures and emotions.

TASTING A GREAT BEER:
A FIVE-COURSE MEAL IN A BOTTLE

There's an old joke that a redneck's seven-course meal is a six-pack and pizza, but as far as I'm concerned a great beer is a five-course meal in a bottle. The first sniff is the salad course, the first small taste is sipped like a soup course, the first big gulp is the appetizer, drinking the main body of the beer is the main course, and when your done, the aftertaste and your general well-being should remind you of a good dessert. Sorry, but you just don't get that from a can of Coorsweiser.

Being a beer enthusiast, I try to restrain myself from drinking a great beer too enthusiastically, and the five-course-meal analogy helps me remember to savor the succulent flavor. Besides, when you pay four dollars for a pint of beer, you want to luxuriate in it for as long as possible. So without further adieu, I'd like to present my surefire method for beer tasting.

First of all, get yourself a nice, tall, clear, wide-mouthed glass. Make sure that it's sparkling clean. I drink ale from ale glasses and lager from lager glasses and mugs, but just find a good clear glass that you like. If you've been eating, clear your palate with some water and a piece of French bread or neutral cracker. Cigarette smoke in your lungs or in the room will diminish your taste and smell, so try to avoid both.

Make sure your beer is the right temperature. A beer that is too cold will not give you a full flavor sensation. I store my beer in the cellar. Except for the hottest months of the summer, cellar temperature is good for full-flavor tasting. If you keep your beer in the refrigerator, I recommend removing it for about an hour to get the optimum flavor. Most beers taste best at forty-five to fifty degrees Fahrenheit. The darker the beer, the warmer it should be.

Examine the beer in the bottle. Hold it up to the light. You can tell a lot about a beer by looking into the bottle. Is there too much air in the neck? This might mean the beer is oxidized and not up to snuff. Is there a ring around the inside of the bottle's neck? This is caused by contamination—return the beer to the store.

Open the beer and listen closely. Does it give a great burp of carbon dioxide (CO_2)? Does it sound flat? This will give you an indication of what's to come.

Does it gush out of the bottle when you open it? This is either old bottle-conditioned beer or has bacterial contamination. Then again, I've had good beer that gushed. (And I don't mean a little blub of foam, I mean *gush!*) Some Belgian beers are outrageously foamy, and if they're not, they've probably been mishandled. It's a judgment call.

Pour the beer down the side of the slightly tipped glass. As the beer pours, tip the glass upward to give yourself two or three fingers of head. If the beer is a super foamy, you might have to wet the inside of the glass first to control the foaming.

If the beer is bottle conditioned, it should say so on the label. Roll the bottle around on the table on its side so as to liquefy the yeast on the bottom. Then pour it straight into the glass (yum!). If you don't like cloudy beer, leave the last half inch in the bottle.

Hold the glass up to the light. Is it the proper color for the style? It shouldn't be cloudy unless it's bottle conditioned. Does the beer have "legs"? That's the visible alcoholic coating that streams down the side of the glass after the beer is swirled. This is usually only visible in high-alcohol beers such as doppelbocks and barley wines.

The First Sniff Is the Salad Course   Swirl the beer in the glass. The carbon dioxide bubbles will release into the air carrying aromatic gases toward your nose. This is the salad course and should be fresh, flowery, refreshing, with a touch of spicy hop herb. The first sniff should be awakening. It whets your appetite for what's to come—like a salad. The first sniff should be consumed heartily, deeply, and with great relish. The bouquet will pass rather quickly and you won't be able to enjoy it as much after a few sniffs. Some beers may be on the tart or sour side and could possibly be compared to a fruit salad.

To further the analogy, the salad may be made of butternut lettuce or romaine. It may have Roma tomatoes or backyard Big Boys. It could be something as simple as iceberg lettuce or something as complicated as a salad bar. Believe it or not, there can be that much variety in the first sniff of a beer. But there's no sneeze guard, and it goes by very quickly.

Clear your mind. Pause. Breathe deep once again.

Make a note of your impressions if you're so inclined. This will come in handy later on when you're trying to remember your favorite beers.

Take a Small Sip-the-Soup Course   The second course is the soup. Like soup, taste it gingerly. A tablespoonful is all you need. Sip it carefully. Roll it around on your tongue. What do you taste? Caramel? Tart? Apples? Molasses? For a full range of flavors that you may taste, see appendix C.

Does it fulfill? Is it nourishing? Does it last? Will it heal? Can it go with you for the rest of the day?

Don't spit! Beer evaluators never spit out the beer like their wine counterparts are known to do. After you swallow, you'll want to judge the beer's aftertaste. The finish is as important as the start.

I can usually tell at this point whether I'm drinking a great beer, a good beer, or a mediocre beer.

The Third Course—The Appetizer   The third course is the pièce de résis-tance. Take another sip, a bigger one. I have a trick in which I sip the beer into my mouth by inhaling ever so slightly—sucking the beer into my mouth. Then, when it's rolling around on my tongue, I *exhale* through my nose. This is absolutely the best way to enjoy beer, but it takes a little practice. Try it without beer first. Warning: Don't try this when you're drunk, as inhaling beer into your lungs can ruin your evening, and possibly the carpet.

Roll the beer around, coating your entire mouth. Is the beer full bodied? Light bodied? What about negatives? Is it astringent? Puckery? Oily?

Chew. Chew the beer while you are swallowing. Exhale up the back of your throat through your nose while chewing. There's olfactory senses there that help you taste. Enjoy every last fulfillment of your senses. Is the beer rich? Is it sustaining? Is it telling you to partake of more?

This part of the tasting could also be likened to a bread course. Because of the grainy nature of barley, many beers have the taste of muffins, toast, burnt toast, pretzels, or wheat bread.

The Fourth Course—The Main Course   Before you begin the fourth course you should put the beer down and clear the palate (unless the brew is so good that you can't stop). At this point, I like to sip some water, chew on a baguette. Cheese? Depends on how serious you are. Cheese stays with you, but it's the perfect complement to a great beer.

After you've cleared the palate, repeat the first three steps. Then enjoy the greater bulk of your liquid refreshment. Wanton abandonment is per-fectly acceptable at this point with a truly great beer.

The Fifth Course—Dessert   The fifth course is dessert. Exhale through the nose. Revel in the candy-sweet high note of the beer. Enjoy your fleet-ing moment of well-being. Be thankful to the people who labor night and day with the nitty-gritty work necessary for beer greatness.

The Finish   The beauty of a five-course beer meal is that you can enjoy more than one per sitting. I never drink the same brand of beer twice in a row. I usually start with the lightest beers and work my way to the darkest. I only drink the ales together and the lagers together, although there's nothing wrong with mixing and matching.

If you are serious about tasting, keep a journal. I can't be serious after three or four beers, but that's part of the fun. When your job is to taste beer, you are working when most people are relaxing. It's tough, but I try to work and play at the same time. Sort of like sipping and sniffing at the same time, it leads to great rewards.

The Top Ten Beers in the World

BEER NUMBER

1

Delirium Tremens
Brouwerij Huyghe
Melle, Belgium

I could have made my life easier. I didn't have to name Delirium Tremens as my number-one favorite beer. If I simply mentioned a beer everyone has heard of, without the name of a drinker's disease, I would get more peace. But that's not what this is all about.

Delirium Tremens is a Belgian lager from the Huyghe Brewery—family owned since 1654. That's in Melle, near the lovely city of Ghent. The name Delirium Tremens speaks for itself. However, I doubt one could get a case of the d.t.'s (if one were so inclined) with much of this stuff around.

Words simply cannot describe the intricate flavor of this beer—but that won't stop me from trying. The color is golden and the head creamy and light. The first sip warms my throat and belly like an old woodstove does a log cabin. It's lightly hopped and surprisingly malty for such an airy, sunshiny beer. With a nose somewhat reminiscent of Orval—another great Belgian ale—the aftertaste is fruity, almost cherry. A warming alcoholic glow works its way down the throat to the stomach. This beer must be sipped slowly so you can revel in each sweet drop. Delirium Tremens has a big body, a rich mouth feel, and a long, sweet aftertaste.

Delirium Tremens is triple fermented. During the principal fermentation the brewers use two different yeasts to get the special taste and high alcohol level. The beer is then lagered for six weeks before mixing with a little candy sugar and bottling. After five weeks' lagering in the bottle, the beer is ready to be sold.

The drawing on the label has pink elephants, dancing crocodiles, and some sort of scaly bird-monster dancing on a full moon. (I didn't even know they had crocodiles in Ghent.) The brewers tell me that the label represents the "three stadia of the illness Delirium Tremens. First you see pink elephants, then green crocodiles appear, and lastly the monstrous bird-creatures invade your mind à la Alfred Hitchcock's *The Birds*." (I had to ask.) The bottle is ceramic dipped, nice and strong in case one were to shakily drop it for some reason.

I held this bottle upside down for a long time to make sure I drained every sweet, creamy drop into my flagon.

BEERSTORY   The most distant ancestors of the Huyghe family began brewing beer in 1654 in Melle, in the same place where the current brewery is situated.

Since 1985, the Huyghe brewery has been exporting beer. They started with France, and today their products are sold all over Europe as well as in the United States, Canada, Argentina, Chile, Japan, and South Korea.

Delirium Tremens was first brewed in December 1988 and presented at the Festival of Ghent in July 1989. The brewery wanted to create a very strong blond beer with a little sweetness.

It was difficult to find a proper name for the new brew. After one long afternoon, though, one of the drinkers said, "If I continue this search while I'm drinking, I will have the delirium tremens." After such comments are great beers named.

The first reaction by the sales reps and others was negative. But the brewers figured, "Either you like it or you don't." I like it, not so much for the name as for the content, which is what beer drinking is all about.

Before World War I, there were three hundred breweries active in Ghent. Today the Huyghe Brewery is the only one left.

FOOD RECOMMENDATIONS   This beer is recommended as an aperitif. Try it with dark bread, cheese, and crackers.

RECOMMENDED RELATED BEERS   The Huyghe Brewery makes several other beers that are great if you can find them. I recommend Sint Idesbald abbey beers, which come in three strengths: Blond, Dubbel, and Triple. The company also brews a sweet, strong, and spicy amber beer called Campus.

SPECIFICATIONS   Delirium Tremens is pricey. I pay $3.99 for an 11.18 oz. (330 ml) bottle. Considering its strength and quality, it's well worth it. The alcoholic content of Delirium Tremens is 9 percent by volume. It's brewed by Brouwerij Huyghe, Brusselsesteenweg 282, B-9000 Melle, Belgium. Telephone: 09 252 15 01. It is imported by Best Brands, Inc., 373 Route 46 West, Building D, Fairfield, NJ 07006. Telephone: (201) 575-6950.

BACKGROUND: A BELGIAN BEER PRIMER

Belgium is ground zero for beer styles. The country has about the same population as New York City yet brews over a thousand different beers. (New York brews less than three dozen.) Until recently, Belgium has more breweries per capita than any other country on the planet.

Some of the most popular Belgian beers are Trappist beers, which are brewed at monasteries. Belgian ales cover the spectrum of beer styles, from fruity, spritzerlike lambic framboise to sour, winy red ale. Entire books have been written about Belgian beers alone. What follows will help you navigate through the sea foam of styles and enjoy some of the truly unique, truly great beers made in Belgium. Most Belgian beers are ales, but lambics are fermented with wild yeast and are a style of beer unto themselves. The Belgian beers listed in this book are Delirium Tremens, Duvel, Chapeau Gueuze Lambic, Lindemans Kriek Lambic, Chimay Peres Trappistes, Corsendonk Monk's Pale Ale, Orval, Saison Dupont, Liefmans Frambozenbier, Rodenbach, Lindemans Gueuze Lambic Cuvée René, Witkap-Pater Abbey Singel Ale, and Kwak.

Belgium has one of the greatest brewing traditions of any country in the world. Until a few years ago, little was known in North America about Belgian beers. A few brave importers began to bring the brews into the United States during the eighties. A few books were written about them, and today Belgian beers are experiencing major growth in the burgeoning beer market.

A few microbrewers have also introduced North America to unique and eccentric Belgian styles—most notably New Belgium Brewing Co. in Fort Collins, Colorado, and Celis in Austin, Texas.

My theory as to Belgium's peculiar hybrid of beer styles has to do with the country's location. Nestled between Germany, with its beer tradition; France, with its wine tradition; and England, with its ale tradition, Belgium seems to have taken the best of all worlds and combined them into beers that can be found nowhere else.

To complicate matters, the small country is divided politically between the Fleming and Walloon nations, each with its own language. I wouldn't want to begin a treatise on Belgian politics here, but suffice it to say that there's a certain competition and a certain pride that each region takes in its beer. Of the nine provinces of Belgium, people in the four northern ones speak Flemish. People in the four southern provinces speak French and are known as Walloons. The province containing Brussels is lingually divided. Confused? Don't be. The Walloons and the Flemish haven't spoken to each other very much for about five hundred years of semi-peaceful coexistence. And that's nothing compared to the ins and outs of Belgian beer.

Brewing in the region that is today's Belgium began as home brewing on farms. In the eleventh century, abbeys began to brew beer commercially—twelve of them are still brewing today. In later years, brewing became a desirable trade, and by the sixteenth century the Belgian Brewers Guild was powerful enough to build the Maison de Brasseurs (Guild Hall of the Brewers) on the Grand Place in Brussels.

Many Belgian beers are treated like fine champagne. They develop their bubbles via *méthode champenoise*, meaning they are bottle conditioned with yeast. Since adding yeast to a finished bottle of beer causes a build up of CO_2 and alcohol, Belgian beers must be corked and wired shut, like champagne. Some finer specimens are wrapped in tissue paper. Upon opening, the outpouring of foam may be so great that it is necessary to wet the sides of the glass first in order to tame the emancipated beer.

As each beer is treated lovingly, most brands have their own special glasses meant for exacting enjoyment. The glasses are usually fine and fluted. (Philistine that I am, I use my Duvel glass to enjoy *any* good beer.)

Perhaps because their brews resemble wine more than beer, Belgians have a highly developed appreciation for the subtleties of their drink. These beers are considered a national treasure but also a "district" specialty. Each town, or even part of a town, has its own way of doing things. Belgium is the crossroads of Europe and has been ruled by everybody from the Romans to the French to the Spanish to the Austrians. No wonder their beer is such a cornucopia of fruit, grapes, barley, spices, and herbs.

Belgium is a beer lover's paradise, but their offerings are a little hard on the pocketbook—unless you're actually in Belgium. Some of their libations are the most expensive beers on the market—almost as expensive as wine. But hey, the best beer in the world only costs as much as a cheap bottle of wine, so let yourself go, give it a try, and most of all, enjoy.

BELGIAN BEER STYLES

Belgian Ale   Belgian ale is copper colored, fruity, yeasty, and smooth. The most famous beer classified as Belgian ale is called Palm, made in a brewery that dates back to 1747. Another famous Belgian ale is De Koninck (the king).

Belgian Red Ale   Belgian red ale is almost burgundy in color and comes from the province of West Flanders. It's sweet on the first taste, sour and tart on the aftertaste. These beers are not for everyone. They are *extremely* sour. This is in part because the beer is aged in wooden barrels, where it picks up caramels, tannins, and acidity more commonly associated with wine.

Belgian Wheat   Belgian wheat, white, or wit (take your pick) is a spicy, orange-flavored beer that resembles Muscat wine as much as beer. It is called *wit*—Flemish for white—because of its cloudiness and pale, straw color. Wits flavored with Curaçao orange peel, coriander, hops, and other spices are called Grand Cru. Wits are usually about fifty percent *unmalted* (raw) wheat, which gives the beer a grainy mouth feel and an apple or plum characteristic.

Wits are bottle conditioned, with a nice pad of yeast on the bottom of the bottle that should be swirled into liquidity after most—but not all—of the beer is poured. Wits can be aged up to six months and are considered perfect accompaniments to dessert.

Belgian Golden Ale   Belgian golden ale can be summed up in one word—Devil. That's because the beer that defines this style is Duvel, a Flemish corruption of the word *devil*. Pronounced "DOO-vl," this beer is a deceptive golden ale that looks and tastes light but weighs in at 8 percent alcohol.

Saison   Saison is Belgian "farmhouse ale," a style originally made for farmers, their families, and their workers. It's a refreshing, citrusy, mild beer with a trademark Belgian rocky, foamy head. Saison is sometimes flavored with star anise and dried orange peels. The beer was originally brewed for the whole family, with potencies running the gambit from "children's strength" to "family," "double," and "royal." It is an ale with a medium body and hearty flavor. There's plenty of resiny hop bite. Saison is refreshing in summer and great with food.

Saison is indigenous to the French-speaking regions of southern Belgium. In the days before refrigeration, all brewing had to be finished by spring, lest wild yeasts and bacteria infect the beer. Saison was brewed in *la saison de mars* (the season of March) to be laid down in wait for summer's heat and fall's harvest. Occasionally, saison was brewed with raw spelt (a type of wheat), oats, or rice. Dupont Saison defines the style.

Trappist Beer   Trappist beers are top-fermented ales. They're pretty strong and bottle conditioned, which gives the imbiber a wonderful layer of healthy yeast at the bottom of the bottle. They have a hardy, unique palate that fairly reeks of their ancient and mystical heritage. Candy sugar is pitched into the kettle, which gives the beer a rummy flavor.

Historically, Trappist beers have been given the greatest respect in Belgium—and now the rest of the world. Today, there are five Trappist

breweries throughout Belgium and one in the Netherlands. These breweries are monasteries in the strictest order and are the only Trappist breweries in the world. Based on the rule of St. Benedict, the Trappist orders
believe in self-sufficiency and living off the land. This task is made easier
by the rather large sums earned from their brewing operation. (Visitors to
the Trappist breweries are often startled to see monks with pagers, cell
phones, fax machines, computers, and all the other trappings of the modern
business world.) Besides beer, monks at Abbaye D'Orval sell over thirty-
five thousand loaves of whole-grain bread and eighty tons of St. Paulin
cheese annually. They also rent rooms to twelve thousand people a year.

Between the abbeys, they produce about twenty beers. Although the
abbeys began brewing between six hundred and eight hundred years ago,
there were various interruptions, and most of them did not begin brewing
in earnest for the modern age until the mid- to late-nineteenth century.

Monks manage all the Trappist breweries, and a few have monks
acting as head brewers. Secular folks do most of the heavy lifting. The
monks are called to prayer at least six times a day but are allowed to have
mild beer with their meals, and most have only one or two glasses. On religious holidays, stronger beer is permitted. Visits to the breweries may be
made by appointment and—sorry ladies—women are forbidden from
entering the cloistered areas where the breweries reside. Nonetheless, over
a hundred thousand people visit Abbaye D'Orval each year.

Abbey Beers   While only the monastery breweries can use the term
Trappist beer, there are several abbeys that license secular breweries to
make beers to their specifications and recipes. Other breweries take inspiration from the Trappist beers and label their products "abbey style." The
abbey styles may have no relationship with any religious order but use a
local shrine or saint as a marketing tool. Abbey beers have similar flavor
profiles as Trappist beers, and some are quite good.

Lambic   Lambics are eccentric and unique. They are made with thirty
percent unmalted wheat and are tart and barely carbonated. Lambic is
brewed with very old hops that have lost their hop bouquet but not their
bittering and preserving qualities. When it is fermented, lambic is left in
large, flat open containers in the attic of the brewery. The windows are
left open, and while the brew is cooling overnight it is visited by wild
yeasts. This sounds quite scary until you realize that the wild yeasts are
from apple blossoms, tulip blooms, and the flowery, fecund Belgian countryside in general. This is such a low dose of yeast that the beer must be

aged in wooden barrels, sometimes for three years, while the wild ones work their magic. Scientists have identified over seventy different yeasts at work in lambic beer. (By the way, this process would give any other brewer a heart attack. Breweries spend considerable time and effort to keep wild yeasts as far from their beer as possible.)

Lambic beer is named after the town of Lambeek, in the Flemish valley of the River Zenne, on the southwest side of Brussels in a district called Payottenland. Lambic was the most popular style of beer in Brussels from the mid-eighteenth century until World War I. Lambics are not everyone's cup of beer, as they are closer to a hard cider than to your common ale. They are sour, winy, and as oddly flavored as they come.

Gueuze   Gueuze (pronounced "gurrs") hits you with twenty-five flavors at once. It's so winelike you can't believe it's beer. This stuff would be a bargain at twice the price.

Gueuze is a beer that blends old and new lambics. The young lambics still have their residual sugars, which set the blended beer to refermenting in the bottle. This gives the beer a geyserlike action when it is released from the bottle. Some believe the word *gueuze* has the same root as the English word *geyser*.

Blending old and young lambics takes great skill and artistry. Flavors must be balanced, undesirable flavors must be covered, and secondary fermentation must take place. Then the blender must decide what proportion of old to young lambics should be used. The more old lambic, the better quality the beer. The gueuze must then be aged to perfection—up to five years.

Faro   Lambics that have been sweetened are called faro. During the height of lambic's popularity before World War I, sour lambics were sold with caramel, molasses, and spice to make them easier for everyday drinking.

Fruit Beer   Some of the most unusual beers in the world are made with fruit. They are tart, dry, pink, and winy. Usually they are malted barley and wheat made into lambic, with raspberries and cherries thrown in. Beers with cherries are called kriek. Beers with raspberries are called framboise or frambozenbier. These beers can please even the most ardent beer hater.

Some of the more eccentric Belgian fruit beers contain peach and banana. American brewers are getting into the fray, offering black currant, cranberry, and apricot fruit beers, among others.

BEER NUMBER

2

Kulmbacher Reichelbräu Eisbock
Reichelbräu Aktien-Gesellschaft
Kulmbach, Germany

Gold Medal, World Champion Eisbock:
World Beer Championship, 1996

Eisbock is the German term for "ice bock beer." Eisbock was probably dis-covered by accident when some hapless brewer's apprentice left his bock beer kegs out-of-doors one cold night. The water in the beer froze, leav-ing behind an alcoholic, delicious beer.

There is a method behind this madness, and freezing is one way to make very strong beer. During the normal brewing process, as beer becomes more alcoholic, it stuns the yeast that is making it so. This kills the goose that lays the golden egg, as it were. Since water freezes at a higher temperature than alcohol, one way to get a potent beer is to freeze it and remove the frozen water. The alcohol stays behind. Reichelbräu is the only brewery in Germany that has made a career out of this tech-nique. It has also registered the name Eisbock as a trademark.

Reichelbräu Eisbock is subtitled Bayrisch G'frorns, or "Bavarian Frozen." It is frozen for sixteen days and then matured for ten weeks in oak casks. Between five and seven percent of the volume remains behind as ice when the brew is removed. This leaves behind a lager that weighs in at 10 percent alcohol by volume.

Eisbock is considered a dessert beer. It contains five malts and three hops. The brew is a thick, rich, malty, deep reddish-brown nectar. There's a sweet malt nose, a remarkably smooth palate, and a hint of whisky-coffee liqueur in the finish.

Please do not confuse this incredible German eisbock with American and Canadian megabrewed products sold under the name ice beer. Calling North American megabeers by this name is like calling fast-food hamburgers chateaubriand.

BEERSTORY   The brewery takes its name from one of its founders, Mr. Reichel. The lagering cellars were cooled by natural ice, which was cut from a lake that used to be on the sight. The lake is gone, but the ice house still stands. In 1970 a new brewhouse was built with an attention-grabbing white tower that is a landmark in Kulmbach.

FOOD RECOMMENDATIONS   This beer is great by itself, as a digestif, or enjoyed with dessert. Bayrisch G'frorns Eisbock can be stirred into a chocolate mousse or even mixed with coffee and brandy.

RECOMMENDED RELATED BEERS   The only commercially brewed *true* eisbock that I know of in North America is called, simply, Eisbock, and is brewed by Niagara Falls Brewing Co., Niagara Falls, Ontario, Canada. It is a limited production, released in early spring, that sells out in a matter of weeks.

SPECIFICATIONS   I paid about $3.99 for an 11 oz. (330 ml) bottle. It's expensive but twice as strong as other beers. The alcoholic content of Reichelbräu Eisbock is 7.9 percent by weight, 10 percent by volume, making it illegal in a few (unenlightened) southern states in America. It is brewed at Reichelbräu Aktien-Gesellschaft, 9 Lichtenfelser Strasse, 8650 Kulmbach, Germany. Telephone: (09221) 7051.

Reichelbräu Eisbock is imported by B. United International, 75 North Central Avenue, Elmsford, NY 10523. Telephone: 914-345-8900. E-mail: 735-5053@mcimail.com.

BACKGROUND: A BOCK PRIMER

Bock beer is a richly flavored, powerful lager with a sweet, malty palate and low hop character. Bocks should be either amber-brown or richly golden. Maibocks are lighter and hoppier, with a bronze-yellow color. Bocks are strong and warming with an alcohol content of at least 5.3 percent by weight, 6.7 percent by volume. They are well aged and generally cold lagered at the beginning of the winter season. *Doppelbock*, or "double bock" may have as much as 11 percent alcohol by weight and 13.5 percent by volume. A delicious triplebock brewed by Samuel Adams has a skyscraping 17.4 percent alcohol by volume, which places it in the *Guinness Book of Records* for the world's strongest beer. Bocks are traditionally released in late February and early March, though Maibock is released for Mayday. Pale bocks should be served at about 45 degrees Fahrenheit, while darker bocks should be served at 50 degrees Fahrenheit. The bocks listed in this book are Reichelbräu Eisbock, Samuel Adams Triple Bock, and Celebrator Doppelbock.

The chill winds of winter may still be blowing outside your window. The gray skies might be opening up, dumping buckets of ice, snow, and rain on your head. But the arrival of bock beers at your bottle shop proves that the promise of spring—once again—is just around the corner.

Crack the cap of any good German bock, pour it in a glass, and your senses are greeted with a massive malt bouquet—rich and caramel. There is very little hop nose and maybe a hint of toasted bread. There is history in that taste. And there's a golden tradition to be savored as the alcohol warmth slides down your throat and protects you from the cold like a woolly old scarf.

The story of bock began in a crystal-clear creek called Crooked Waters, a tributary of the Ilm River near Einbeck, Lower Saxony, Germany. The waters may be crooked, but their purity and goodness made Einbeck one of the first international brewing centers in Europe. Einbeck was exporting its beer as long ago as the eleventh century, and records prove that it was happily received in such far-off lands as Russia, Norway, England, and Jerusalem. Einbeck licensed and taxed citizen brewers at a time when the brewer's art was only practiced by monks and under royal command. It didn't hurt Einbeck's reputation to have its beer enjoyed by Martin Luther—on the day of his wedding.

The name *bock* is an interesting mixture of malaprops and fancy, where mangled German meets a rutting billy goat on the road to serendipity.

By the mid-1500s the beer of Einbeck was very popular in Munich-which was itself a brewing center. Munichers in the know asked for *einbeckischbier*, or beer imported from Einbeck. After several hardy drafts, the name inevitably got shortened and corrupted to *ein beck* or *ein bock* in the Bavarian accent. Soon enough, the name stuck, and bock was the name consigned to the style.

Now it just so happens that *bock* also means "male goat" in German. And what could be better than the rutting billy goat as a symbol of spring and strong drink? The billy goat has long been a symbol of fertility and even lechery. Early ads, labels, and posters for bock beer showed a lascivious, leering goat—sometimes in *liederhosen*. The goat is also known for its powerful kick, another happy coincidence associated with bock beer.

On a more pious note, bock beer was traditionally released before Lent. Lenten fasting rules prohibited partaking of meat or wine but left a loophole when it came to beer. Many a devout worshiper made it through the Lenten fast with only bock beer for sustenance.

Eventually the bock style became so important that its qualities were written into law. Today's German bock beers must have an alcohol content of at least 6.7 percent by volume. The color has been deemed to be either amber-brown or golden but not in between.

When Bavarians were on their way to becoming world-class brewers, a blessing of the yeast was taking place in the caves where the beer was stored. Deep in the dark mountain caves, a cold-loving yeast developed all by itself. This yeast, later known as lager yeast, gave less of a spicy, fruity flavor (associated with ale). This allowed the well-rounded, sweet malt bouquet and flavor of the beer to come to the fore. Lager yeast also tolerated alcohol better, thus allowing stronger brews to be made.

Munich has become the bock beer center of Germany. Every year on May Day the prime minister of Bavaria and the mayor of Munich tap the season's first barrel of Maibock. Some well-known Munich bock brewers are Paulaner, Augustiner, and Spatan. All started out as breweries run by monks, some as early as 1328.

Bock beer was practically unheard of in ale-loving America until millions of German immigrants brought it with them shortly before the Civil War. Unfortunately, German-American brewers also adopted the American practice of using corn or rice as adjuncts in their beer. After Prohibition, large breweries passed off as bock corn-laden pilsner with caramel coloring added. Most bock made by large American breweries today is little better.

Somehow, Americans got it into their heads that bock beer was made from the dregs of fermentation tanks and that the tanks were only cleaned once a year, in spring. This rumor was perpetuated by people obviously ignorant of brewing techniques—brewers keep their kettles and kegs spot-less, cleaning them thoroughly after each brew, lest ambient yeasts and bacteria contaminate the next batch.

As the American craft-beer revolution gained a foothold in the marketplace, most small breweries were not equipped to make bock beer. Fortunately for us, some micros bit the bullet and became lager based, which cost them more in terms of beer storage and cold refrigeration temps. A few micros even import German-speaking brewers from Weinhenstephan—the world's oldest brewing college.

Every spring in Milwaukee, Wisconsin, microbrewers participate in the "Blessing of the Bock." The ceremony is led by Lakefront Brewery and supported by Baderbräu, New Glarus, Cherryland, Appleton, Capital, MidCoast and other breweries. A priest of the local Catholic church blesses the bock from an old book of Roman Catholic rituals. After the blessing, serious drinking ensues.

DOPPELBOCK   Lager yeast is more tolerant of alcohol than ale—it doesn't die off as quickly when beer becomes more spirituous. This allowed clever brewers to develop *doppelbock*, or "double bock." While not really double the strength of bock, why mince words when talking about something as powerful, thick, chewy, and delicious as doppelbock?

The first doppelbock was brewed by the Paulaner Brewery in Munich in 1780. Paulaner was a former monastery brewery. In that spirit, the company began another tradition by naming their strong, dark lager Salvator, or "Savior." Ever after, any company brewing a doppelbock ended the name with the suffix -*ator*. This has given the world such lovely beer cognomen as Celebrator, Optimator, Navigator, Animator, and Kulminator. It has also given us such humbling names as Terminator.

Brewpubs have a harder time making bock than regular ales and lagers. Bock takes up to eight weeks of storage in near-freezing temperatures. Doppelbock can require up to six months' storage, an impossibility for small brewers with small profit margins. Some brew a doppelbock with ale yeast and have success with an unusual and often delicious hybrid. American bocks tend to be less alcoholic than their German cousins.

MAIBOCKS   A golden-colored, more hoppy bock is called a *maibock*, or *ur-bock* (*mai* as in the month of "May," and *ur* meaning "original"). Maibocks, also known as pale bocks, are more refreshing than regular bocks and are meant to be enjoyed during the warmer, sunnier days of May. Maibock has a distinctly hoppy nose and bitter finish. A couple of American micros brew decent maibocks.

BEER NUMBER

3

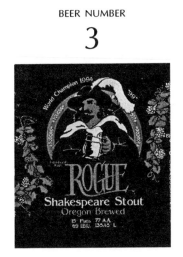

Rogue Shakespeare Stout
Rogue Ales
Newport, Oregon

Platinum Medal: World Beer Championship, 1994
Gold Medal: World Beer Championship, 1995
Gold Medal: California Beer Festival, 1995

The company slogan is, "Dedicated to the rogue in all of us." What scribe of beer would not love a brew named after the Bard himself? But a Rogue by any other name is still a Rogue. These folks out in Newport, Oregon—besides living in one of the most beautiful places on the West Coast—crank out the most consistently fantastic beer in America.

Shakespeare Stout is ebony-night in color. Poured straight and fast, it develops a good head. It smells exactly true-to-stout style with undertones of seagoing crustaceans. You could eat the head with a spoon, it's so creamy and rich. And its got a hell of a great bitter piquancy! Sir Shakespeare has lots of tart West Coast hop-bitter palate with very little floral nose. There's oats in them thar beer, which gives it an earthy flavor and silky texture. Takes "dry" to new heights, a result, no doubt, of Rogue's proprietary "Pacman" yeast, which reduces simple sugars and leaves complex ones. Thick, rich, tart, and dry, as beautifully blended as the blue and purple label, with a final taste of chocolate. What's not to love about it? This is one beer I can't put down.

The Bard of Beer is made with nine ingredients, which help add to its complexity. There are 33.5 percent specialty grains and the total malt adds up to .45 pounds of grain per 22 oz. bottle. The water is free-range coastal water, and it's topped by an oxygen-absorbing cap which leeches out any stale flavors that might develop during shipping. These folks care greatly about quality and yet sell their brews at a competitive price. To quote their publicity material: "We remember it is not simply a matter of profit but a highly personal work of art." Hallelujah!

BEERSTORY   Rogue Ales began in 1989 with an 800-square-foot brewery and a 1,000-square-foot pub on the working bayfront of Newport, Oregon. It was, and still is, a place where tourists can rub elbows with fishermen and other native Oregonians. The brewery was started by Jack Joyce, a former vice president of Nike.

In 1992, with demand growing for Rogue Ales, the brewery moved across the bay, into an old shipbuilding warehouse. A third location dubbed the House of Rogue/International Association of Rogues Headquarters opened near the brewery in 1995.

Brewmaster John Maier began his work career as a senior electronics engineer for Hughes Aircraft Co. He brewed his first batch of home brew in 1981 and soon found himself in the role of masterbrewer in the expanding Pacific Northwest microbrewing industry. After graduating from Siebel Institute of Technology, a brewing school in Chicago, John went to work in the Alaskan Brewery in Juneau. That same month he walked in during the very first brewing of Rogue Ales in Oregon, where he was persuaded to work. The rest is Rogue-story. This guy is hot. He's got more medals than you can load in a beer barrel. He's won world championships and gold medals at the Great American Beer Festival. His beers have been shown at the Great British Beer Festival and been included in displays at the Smithsonian Institution.

FOOD RECOMMENDATIONS   It's worth a trip to Newport, Oregon, to visit the Rogue Ales Public House or the House of Rogues for a beer by the sea. The brewpubs sell Rogue fresh from the brewery along with such taste treats as barley-crust pizza, Cornish pastries, ale bread, and beer-soaked sausages. Also recommended with Pacific shellfish and fish.

RECOMMENDED RELATED BEERS   These folks don't make a bad beer—and they make a lot of different styles, so you'll never get bored. Here in no particular order are the Rogue beers I recommend: Mocha Porter, St. Rogue Red Ale, American Amber Ale, Cran-n-Cherry Ale, Hazelnut Brown Nectar, Oregon Golden Ale, Rogue-n-Berry Ale, Mexicali Rogue (chili pepper beer), Maierbock Ale, Mo Ale (hefe-weizen), Mogul Ale (strong ale), Dead Guy Ale (Octoberfest style), McRogue Scotch Ale, Imperial Stout, Smoke Ale, Old Crustacean Barleywine.

SPECIFICATIONS   I've seen 22 oz. (650 ml) bottles of Rogue Ales sold from $2.99 to $3.99 per bottle. The alcoholic content of Shakespeare Stout is 6.10 percent by volume. Shakespeare Stout is brewed by Rogue Ales. Their mailing address is 3135 SE Ferry Slip Road, Newport, OR 97365. Telephone: 541-867-4131. E-mail: rogue@pstat.com. Web page: http//realbeer.com/rogue.

BACKGROUND: A STOUT PRIMER

Stouts are rich, black, and roasty, with creamy tan heads. They are incredibly complex ales with slight burnt malt notes and hints of molasses in the finish. Stouts come in five styles: Dry stout, imperial stout, oatmeal stout, sweet stout, and milk or cream stout, which has lactic sugar (lactose) added. Traditionally, dry stouts are Irish and sweet stouts are English. Most American microbrewed stouts are of the dry Irish variety. Guinness Stout is the world's most famous stout—as well it should be; Guinness invented the style in the early nineteenth century. Today, any American ale microbrewery worth its malt should produce a drinkable stout. Stouts are darker, richer, hoppier, and more alcoholic than porters, the style on which they are based. Stouts are about 5 percent alcohol by volume. The stouts in this book are Shakespeare Stout, Grant's Imperial Stout, Murphy's Irish Stout, Guinness Stout, Samuel

Smith's Imperial Stout, Samuel Smith's Oatmeal Stout, Pyramid Espresso Stout, Oasis Zoser Oatmeal Stout, Redhook Doubleblack Stout, and Barney Flats Oatmeal Stout.

Technological advances in malting techniques in the early nineteenth century allowed malt to be roasted to a deep brown or black color. Using a drum roaster much like a coffee roaster, the high-temperature process was patented in 1817. This black patent malt gives stout its inky color and roasty, toasty coffeelike flavor.

Today hundreds of American microbreweries produce their own unique take on the stout style. Redhook has gone so far as to make a stout containing Starbuck's coffee, which is the ultimate statement. Excellent stouts come from all three American coasts—Pacific, Atlantic, and the oh-so-odd Third Coast of the Great Lakes.

Dry Stout   Dry stout has scads of hop bitterness and is as black as night. One would expect such an imposing beer to be difficult to drink, but dry stouts, especially when served on tap, are smooth and silky and can be drunk practically like water. The secret behind the smoothness of dry Irish stout is the nitrogen charge, as opposed to carbonation. Many American pubs do not want to have Murphy's Irish Stout or Guinness Stout on tap because the brewers insist that their beer be charged with nitrogen, which is smooth and lacks the acidic bite of carbon dioxide. It also means different tanks and fittings for the bar. Today both Guinness and Murphy's come in a can with a tiny plastic widget filled with nitrogen. When opened the nitrogen shoots into the beer and makes it look like black whipped cream when poured. It goes down about as easy as whipped cream, and I'd have to say that while I usually eschew beer in cans, those nitrogen widgets make it worth putting up with the aluminum. Murphy's has taken it one step further by adding the widget to dark brown bottles of Murphy's Irish Stout. Now that's progress!

Microbrewed American dry stouts do not have the nitrogen, but a few add secret ingredients like peat-smoked malt or molasses that give them a unique and complex blend that is to die for.

Sweet Stout   In the old days, folks who wanted a sweet stout simply stirred a spoonful of sugar into the already rich dry stout. Some even considered it a health drink. Brewers, always looking for a new taste, began making sweet stouts in the late nineteenth century. Most are low in alcohol, at about 3.5 percent by volume. Sweet stouts labeled as such are difficult to find in America, but oatmeal stouts tend to be on the sweet side and are more widely available.

Milk Stout   In 1875 a gentleman named John Johnson sought a patent for an invention that he called milk beer. Johnson was a lawyer representing the inventors—a doctor and two chemists. These folks envisioned a beer made from whey, milk, lactose, and hops. As disgusting as that may sound, anyone who has had a White Russian or Irish cream liqueur might see the point. Others may remember the German beer style Berliner weisse, which uses lactic yeast strains to give the beer a cloudy, milky texture.

Back in nineteenth-century England, other folks got the idea that a milk stout would be medicinal, have food value, and be less gassy. In 1907 the Mackeson brewery in Hythe, Kent, made its first batch of milk stout by adding lactose—which does not ferment—to the beer.

By 1936, Mackeson Milk Stout was widely available. Other stouts, known as cream stouts, soon followed. The label of Mackeson boasted, "Each pint contains the energizing carbohydrates of ten ounces of pure dairy milk." This claim was later removed, but the beer, being low in alcohol, was considered a restorative for the sick and invalid, it was also recommended for nursing mothers. After World War II, the British government forced brewers to remove the milk and cream language from the beer labels.

While there are still a few beers that use the word *cream* in their labels—most notably Samuel Adams Cream Stout, Watney's Cream Stout, and Little Kings Cream Ale—they are not made with lactose.

Oatmeal Stout   Long ago and far away, brewers used whatever grains were handy to make beer. Transportation networks were undeveloped, and reliable delivery of barley couldn't always be counted on. Thus it was many a batch of beer that had oats thrown in to fill out the need for fermentable sugars.

During the health craze of the late nineteenth century, oatmeal once again became a desirable ingredient in stout. For about seventy-five years several British breweries made oatmeal stouts. Eldridge Pope quit making the last one in 1975. But in 1980 beer importer Charles Finkel of Merchant du Vin in Seattle persuaded the Samuel Smith Brewery in Yorkshire to revive the style. Since then several British breweries and a few North American micros have begun pitching oats into their mashes.

Oats are hard to brew with because they turn into gelatinous glue when mashed. But the effort provides the beer with a full body, a smooth finish, and a nutty taste on top of the already complex stout flavor.

Imperial (Russian Stout)   As far as I'm concerned, imperial stout is the best beer style in the world. If it was good enough for Russian tsars, it's good enough for me. (There, I said it.)

The winters in Russia are dark, unbearably cold, and long. Folks up there don't mess around when it comes to drink. Imperial stout is stout times two. It's strong (9.5 percent to 10.5 percent alcohol by volume), black, and roasty. Fermented at warm temperatures to a high-alcohol potency, imperial stouts are robust and intricate in flavor. The fruitiness is burnt, and the black color reminds the tongue that there is a flavor of sweet tar for the tsar—more licorice really. The aftertaste reminds one of coffee, sherry, and perhaps a good cigar.

Imperial stout started life as a strong porter in London's great breweries, circa 1780. At that time the porter, labeled XXXXX to denote its strength, was shipped to Germany, Scandinavia, Kaliningrad, and other Baltic ports of call. The original brewer of imperial stout was the London-based Anchor Brewery, which exported the stuff until the eve of World War I. In the old days, imperial stout was aged at the brewery for eighteen to twenty-four months. Today's imperial stouts are aged about one year.

BEER NUMBER

4

Duvel
Brasserie Moortgat
Flanders, Belgium

Sweet and light, but watch out, because Duvel means "devil" in Flemish. I take that as a warning. As a matter of fact, this is a deceptively power-ful ale. Only a true, though slightly perverse, brewing artist could so effi-ciently extract the sweetest sugars from the barley and convert them into candy rocket fuel.

This is the quintessential strong ale that's renowned for its complex-ity and depth of flavor. In Belgium, Duvel is treated as sort of a barley Jagermeister, served in frosted glasses, icy cold. The brew is honey-golden in color and foamy as all get out. The head is Olympian and as roiled up as the sea on a windy, crystal-blue day. The bouquet tickles the nose from the inside like a feather. It's infused with carbonation and possesses the unique Belgian flavor of antique leather and clubby velveteen smoking rooms. The rich rocky head leaves the classic "Belgian lace" on the glass's side, and there's a hint of pear in the aftertaste.

This is one of Belgium's secular brewers as you might have guessed by the name of the beer—no monk would call a beer Duvel. The malt is grown in France, and it has that southern sunshine, golden quality that is so forthright in the beer. It must be the most golden barley grown on the planet because the beer is extremely light in body and color while retaining its kick. Without a doubt, Duvel uses only the highest quality "noble" hops available on the continent. The Saaz and Styrian Goldings hops are a one-two knockout of bouquet and bitter. Their perfume distracts you from what is to follow—a jarring alcohol punch! Whew! These guys know something that no one else does!

The reason for Duvel's unsurpassed character is the painstaking, labor-intensive triple-fermentation process that is unique to the brewery. A sign on the brewery in massive red letters says "Ssssh . . . Duvel is ripening here." This bottle conditioning gives Duvel the champagne sparkle that makes it one of the world's best beers. The beer is stabilized in bottles for six weeks in cold storage before its release, and Duvel aficionados like to store it in their basements for up to three months to further blend.

BEERSTORY   Duvel has Scotch blood in its background. Between the two world wars, the great Belgian brewing scientist Jean de Clerck "took apart" a bottle of McEwan's Scotch Ale under a microscope. At the time, McEwan's was bottle conditioned with a mix of ten to twenty different strains of living yeast. De Clerck did the work with a local brewery owned by the Moortgat family. With the yeast from McEwan's, the Moortgat brewery introduced a new dark strong ale. When the brew was sampled, a brewery worker said it was "a devil of a beer!" The brewery decided to call it Duvel.

In 1970, the Moortgat Brewery introduced a golden version of Duvel. The legend spread far and wide, and today Duvel is one of the most enthusiastically consumed beers in the world.

Duvel is imported by Vanberg & Dewulf, whose passion for the beers of Belgium and the North of France has been their business since 1982. They import thirty great beers from ten breweries in eighteen styles.

FOOD RECOMMENDATIONS   Duvel became popular at the Belgian seaside and is a classic accompaniment to seafood. The importer recommends Duvel with shellfish and with ocean fish such as monkfish and salmon. Belgians cook with Duvel as well—such dishes as *Waterzooi* (chicken, celery, and carrot stew, enriched with cream and Duvel). Any recipe that calls for beer will taste better with Duvel.

RECOMMENDED RELATED BEERS   There are other golden Belgian ales, but none so singular as Duvel.

SPECIFICATIONS   I pay about $2.50 for a 12 oz. (355 ml.) bottle of Duvel, which is 8.5 percent alcohol by volume. Duvel is brewed at the Brasserie Moortgat, Breendonkdorp 58, B-2870, Breendonk-Puurs, Belgium. Telephone: (03) 886 71 21. Duvel is imported by Vanberg & Dewulf, 52 Pioneer Street, Cooperstown, NY 13326. Telephone: 607-547-8184.

BEER NUMBER

5

Caledonian Golden Pale (Organic)
Caledonian Brewing Company, Ltd.
Edinburgh, Scotland

Caledonian Golden Pale pours very golden and perfectly foamy. The smell of Kent hop perfume wafts right out along with the sweet smell of Scottish malt. The beer is light, well balanced, rich, and delicious. The organic ingredients have a certain cleanliness and wholesomeness that is both reassuring and refreshing. The neck label informs me that the organic barley and Kentish hops have been guaranteed by the British Soil Association. The back label explains the natural method of sustainable agriculture used in the growing of the ingredients.

The sweet bouquet of the hops hits the nose with every sip, and about halfway through, I get a subtle hint of peat smoke and fresh Atlantic seas. This ale is ultimately drinkable and made with the utmost care and skill.

I appreciate a brewery that goes to the extra time and expense necessary to produce a great ale using organic elements. Very notable.

BEERSTORY   The history of the Caledonian Brewery harkens back to one frigid Friday the thirteenth, of January 1865, in Edinburgh, Scotland. On that unlucky day, George Lorimer died in a fire at the city's Theatre Royal. George left a wife and four children behind. One of the children was George Jr., the oldest son who, at the age of eighteen, was left to support the family. George Jr. was determined to go into the brewing business. Accordingly, in October 1869, George Lorimer Jr. purchased a piece of land on the western outskirts of Edinburgh and began to construct the Caledonian Brewery. He went into partnership with Robert Clark, head brewer at one of Edinburgh's largest breweries. The brewery had its own wells and malt house and a cooperage to build barrels. Caledonian "Scotch" ales became popular, and George managed the brewery for forty-nine years, until 1918. He died in 1939.

The Caledonian Brewery happily continued to fulfill its mission, celebrating its centennial anniversary in 1969. By then the cooperage and malt house had been closed. In 1986, there were only a handful of breweries left in Edinburgh, down from thirty in the earlier years. A large English company gained control of Caledonian and announced its closure. Local people were appalled, and with the help of some local politicians, the financial community, and the brewery staff, the brewery was bought and saved.

The availability of Caledonian beers had been limited for years. With a new lease on life, new products were launched by the brewery. Today, Caledonian has become a vital part of the British brewing scene, and their direct-fired brewing coppers, a system that was installed in 1869, are the last still in use anywhere.

One of the brewery's saviors was Russell Sharp, a former distiller for Chivas Regal. Using his native knowledge of malting and distilling, Sharp's touch has made Caledonian's ales some of the most popular in Scotland. A new pub, called Caledonian Ale House and Bistro, has recently been added to the front of the brewery and is serving bottled, draft, and cask-conditioned Caley ales. Highly recommended!

FOOD RECOMMENDATIONS   This pale ale makes a great pairing with almost any food. I recommend drinking it with roast beef or chicken, smoked salmon, fresh crab, steak, barbecue, or such spicy Eastern cuisines as Szechwan, East Indian, and Malaysian.

RECOMMENDED RELATED BEERS   Caledonian makes MacAndrew's Scotch Ale, listed elsewhere in this book, along with the organic Golden Promise Ale and Double Dark Ale.

SPECIFICATIONS   I pay about $2.99 for 17 oz. (500 ml) bottles of Golden Pale. The alcoholic content is about 5 percent by volume. Golden Pale is brewed at The Caledonian Brewing Co., Slateford Road, Edinburgh EH11, 1PH, Scotland. Telephone: (031) 337 1286. The Caledonian Ale House is at 1-3 Haymarket Terrace, Edinburgh. Telephone: 01 31 337 1006. It is imported by Best Brands, Inc., 373 Route 46 West, Building D, Fairfield, NJ 07006. Telephone: 201-575-6950.

BACKGROUND: A PALE ALE PRIMER

Pale ale was originally the name given to "bitter in a bottle," as opposed to "bitter in a cask." Today it has evolved into its own style. Pale ale is dry, with a fruity, complex palate. It's honey gold to amber red, with a nutty malt character, a noticeable hop bitterness, a subtle hop bouquet, and a long hop finish. Centuries ago, when most beer was muddy brown in color, pale meant lighter than that standard but not pale as in today's American pilsner. Pale ale has an alcohol content of about 5 percent by volume.

India pale ale, or IPA, was the name given to the beer that followed British soldiers and bureaucrats when they colonized India. The beer had to be well hopped to preserve it across an ocean journey that took many weeks. The beer also had to be alcoholically strong to survive. Today IPA is the "premium" version of the pale ale style. The pale ales listed in this book are Caledonian Golden Pale, Royal Oak Pale Ale, and Samuel Smith's Pale Ale.

Contrary to popular belief, crystal-clear sparkling beer was first achieved in British pale ale, not Bohemian pilsner lager. This accomplishment coincided with the growing popularity of bottled beer. Put the two together and you have a premier British style called pale ale.

Back at the turn of the nineteenth century, the world's beer was brown, yeasty, and cloudy. As a matter of fact, you could cut it with a knife. Now there's nothing wrong with dark, cloudy beer. But to have a beer that visually resembled champagne—well, that was something. It was a little bit of home-grown opulence for the growing nouveau riche British middle classes.

Before long the name *pale ale* was used for any amber to copper-red bitter style that was in a bottle. Bottled beer too was considered a sophisticated luxury in the early 1800s. One didn't have to go to a smoky pub and rub elbows with the great unwashed to have a good ale in a bottle.

The first pale ale was produced in London in the 1750s, but the style quickly became associated with the brewing town of Burton-on-Trent, in England's Midlands. Monks first began brewing in the Trent Valley in the 1200s. Even in those ancient days, the water of Burton was known to be of a high quality unique for brewing.

The wells of Burton—some one thousand feet deep—are drilled through sandstone, which gives their waters a high quantity of gypsum. This calcium sulfate causes magical chemical reactions during mashing and yeast development. It also adds a hardness to the water that gives the beer a firm body and dryness that is characteristic of a pale ale style. Pale ale brewers elsewhere add "Burton salts" to their water to achieve the same effect. Some English beer labels claim their beers are "Burtonized."

The first pale ale developed in Burton was at the Allsopp Brewery. The family that owned the brewery had been making beer in the area since the Crusades. Legend has it that the head brewer at Allsopp mixed the first batch of pale ale in a teapot.

Perhaps Burton's most famous pale ale is brewed by Bass. The impetus behind Bass's early rise to fame could be found in their unique brewing system called Burton Unions, which, sadly, was discontinued in the 1980s. The eccentric Burton Unions brewing system used rows of wooden barrels to ferment the beer. The barrels were connected with bent (swan-necked) tubes to long open troughs. As the yeast bubbled and frothed, it would force the ale, by natural carbon dioxide pressure, up into the series of open troughs. For three or four days, the foamy beer circulated like the tides, ebbing and flowing through the great hall of shiny troughs. After the yeast had worked its magic and settled back down, the ale would run back into the barrels. This "training" of the yeast made it individualistic and gave it a peerless fruity character, with a hint of apple in the nose. Much of the yeast was left behind in the troughs, where it could easily be gathered for the next batch.

This weird, open system was a way to ease the pressure on the barrels at a time when exploding barrels at a brewery could kill or drown people. (Anyone who has ever shaken up a beer can knows that CO_2 can pack a lot of pressure.) And, yes, people really have drowned in beer. Of course, explosions were the most drastic examples—and memorable in beer history. Usually the overflowing yeast would simply make a sticky mess and put the beer at risk for contamination.

To the beer world's continuing sadness, the Burton Unions labor-intensive method of brewing was discontinued by Bass in the early 1980s, before the modern beer revolution reared its hoppy head. The system was almost two hundred years old and a costly nightmare to maintain. But the living yeast was also two centuries old.

The independent Marston's Brewery in Burton still uses a modified Burton Unions system in its excellent Pedigree Bitter Ale.

India Pale Ale (IPA)   Anybody could take a keg of ale and ship it on a clipper ship across the ocean. But not many people could drink that ale when it disembarked. If you were to send scholars and soldiers, holy men and bakers to a far-flung tropical land, you damn well better send some good beer to sustain them. India pale ale was made for such a purpose.

Burton was developing its world-class brewing heritage long before it was connected to the rest of England by decent road or rail. It was the era of river and canal shipping, and it was almost as easy to float beer to India as it was to London.

Export beers were made with a very high alcohol content to survive the journey. They would continue to ferment on the way and arrive in distant lands in peak condition. They were also extremely well hopped so that the preservative properties in the skunky flower would keep the beer in tip-top shape. And when I say well hopped, I mean approximately *five times* the hopping rate of today's IPAs. The brain puckers at the thought. Of course, these hops might have been aged—dried out—to reduce their bitterness, but not their anti-infectant qualities.

Be that as it may, India pale ale became a hit in the homelands as well. And while today no British brewery produces an IPA with the strength or bitterness of Victorian IPAs, the revolutionary Americans—always known for excesses—certainly have tried their hand at it.

Ballantine Ale was one of the last commercially brewed pale ales in America before the microbrewery revolution. Originally brewed by the Scotsman Peter Ballantine in 1830, Ballantine IPA inspired many of today's microbrewers when they were still making ale in their kitchens. The brand bounced from Albany to Newark to Rhode Island. Today, Ballantine is owned by Pabst and made who knows where. I sampled some recently, and, while tasting faintly of corn, still contained a glimmer of its former greatness.

Of course pale ale and IPA have become stock-in-trade for most of America's craft brewers. Check in with your local brewpub or micro-brewery, and chances are good that you will find a fresh, locally produced pale ale or IPA worthy of its legend. And don't forget to try the British pale ales as well.

BEER NUMBER

6

Chapeau Gueuze Lambic
Brouwerij de Troch
Wambeek, Belgium

Gold Medal: BTI World Beer Championship, 1994

This is one of the world's best gueuze lambics. It's spontaneously fermented with natural airborne yeast and aged in oak casks. It's oaky, smoky, winy, and more complex than simple words can describe. Chapeau Gueuze is a deep, fecund forest in a green glass bottle—leathery and indescribably delicious. No bad aftertastes and all great foretaste. The naturally occurring yeast brings out the mossy oak flavor in a very palatable way. This lambic has a pepper nose and a vanilla-fruit flavor that reeks of ancient Europe.

The beer is unfiltered, and refermented in the bottle.

BEERSTORY   De Troch brewery is located east of Brussels in the town of Wambeek. It's a small, family-owned brewery.

FOOD RECOMMENDATIONS   Good with mussels and flavorful cheeses, or try as an aperitif in place of sherry.

RECOMMENDED RELATED BEERS   De Troch makes some fruit lambics under the Chapeau label that are unique. Try their banana, pineapple, cherry, raspberry, plum, peach, and strawberry lambics.

SPECIFICATIONS   Chapeau Gueuze is about $4.98 for a 12.7 oz. (375 ml) bottle. It can be aged for two years. The alcoholic content is 4.1 percent by volume. Chapeau is brewed by Brouwerij de Troch, 20 Lange Straat, B-1741 Wambeek, Belgium. Telephone: 02 582 10 27. It is imported by All Saint's Brands, 201 Main Street SE, No. 212, Minneapolis, MN 55414. Telephone: 800-587-9272.

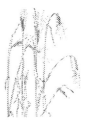

BEER NUMBER

7

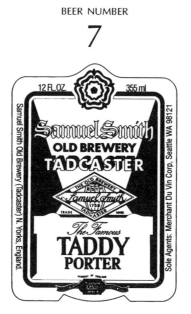

Samuel Smith's Taddy Porter
Samuel Smith Old Brewery
Tadcaster, North Yorkshire, England

One of the best porters in the world, Taddy Porter is deep ruby-black and has a toasty, delicate aroma with a slight hint of butterscotch. It's tart and tangy and slightly salty with a long coffee finish. You can almost taste the North Sea in this beer. And if you close your eyes, you can see the heather-covered hills of the breathtaking English coast. This beer defines the porter style.

Taddy Porter has won awards from Campaign for Real Ale and as the Import Beer of the Year.

BEERSTORY   Samuel Smith, founded in 1758, is the oldest brewery in Yorkshire, England. The village of Tadcaster, where it is located, is also the home of brewing giants Bass and Courage. Samuel Smith's is still a family-owned brewery—and Charles Dickens described it in A Tale of Two Cities. Their commitment to old-fashioned quality is world reknowned.

The Samuel Smith Old Brewery brews its beer using huge slate fermenters called Yorkshire Squares. The Yorkshire Squares contribute to

Taddy Porter's matchless character. The squares are giant open brewing vats, the sides of which are made from single slabs of slate. Yorkshire's slate was once quarried to make the streets of London as well as to make fermenters for many English breweries.

The slate fermenters, which are about twelve foot square, impart a soft roundness to the beer's character that can be found nowhere else. That is why the name Samuel Smith keeps popping up in this book.

The yeasts bred in the Yorkshire Square system give the beer its almost buttery flavor. The squares are stacked. As the ale ferments in the lower square, it rises into the upper square. The yeast residue stays behind, and the ale sinks back into its original slate square tank. These distinctive Yorkshire yeasts do not ferment the beer as efficiently as some, which gives Sam's a satisfying full body.

Taddy Porter is imported by Merchant du Vin, America's leading specialty beer distributor. The import company was founded in 1978 when America had only forty breweries. Merchant du Vin has been responsible for introducing many classic brewing styles that have become a staple on the beer lover's menu.

FOOD RECOMMENDATIONS   Taddy Porter is famous as an accompaniment to oysters on the half shell or oysters Rockefeller. Also good with clams, mussels, crab cocktail, lobster bisque, and other shellfish. Goes with veal and can be served as a dessert over vanilla ice cream, or with chocolate if you dare! Serve at 55 degrees Fahrenheit.

RECOMMENDED RELATED BEERS   Every single beer made at Samuel Smith's Old Brewery is a classic, and several of their beers may be found elsewhere in this book. I recommend Samuel Smith's Oatmeal Stout, Imperial Stout, Nut Brown Ale, Old Brewery Pale Ale, Winter Welcome Ale, and Pure Brewed Lager Beer.

SPECIFICATIONS   Samuel Smith's Taddy Porter is about $3 for a 18.2 oz. (550 ml) bottle, about $9 for a six-pack of 12 oz. bottles. The alcoholic content of Taddy Porter is 4 percent by weight, 5.13 percent by volume. Samuel Smith's Taddy Porter is brewed at The Old Brewery, Tadcaster, Yorkshire, LS24 9DSB, England. Telephone: (0937) 832 225. It is imported by Merchant du Vin, 140 Lakeside Avenue, Seattle, WA 98122-6538. Telephone: 206-322-5022. E-mail: info@mdv-beer.com.

BACKGROUND: A PORTER PRIMER

Porter is an intensely flavored, full-bodied beer brewed from roasted, unmalted barley, chocolate malt, and black patent malt. It has a roasty-toasty palate with flavors ranging from dark chocolate to coffee-mocha. Some porters may be very bitter. The color may range from dark ruby-brown to almost black, but not quite as black as stout. Traditional porters are dry, but some microbrewed porters may be on the sweet side. Porters are not necessarily high in alcohol and range from 4 percent to 7 percent alcohol by volume. The porters included in this book are Samuel Smith's Taddy Porter, Geary's London Style Porter, and Left Hand Black Jack Porter.

Porter started out in the early 1700s in England as a sort of a throw-it-in-the-glass-style beer. Carters and haulers from London's Victoria Station would ask their barman to simply pour a little pale ale, some brown ale, and some old ale into one glass. This libation proved one couldn't have too much of a good thing. It was called an "Entire." In 1722 a fellow named Ralph Harwood decided to brew a ready-made Entire. Instead of calling it a "Harwood," he honored his best customers by calling it "porter." Like many beer fads before and since, the brewing giants of the time picked up the idea and began to brew their own porters.

By the 1760s the Industrial Revolution was moving into high gear, and breweries like Whitbread were building huge factories that specialized in porter. As populations in London increased, brewers began to store huge quantities of porters in giant wooden tubs called porter tuns. One brewery was reputed to have a porter tun so large as to seat two hundred people for a sit-down dinner.

As England's world influence grew, its beer styles traversed the oceans. By the beginning of the nineteenth century, today's famous Guinness Brewery in Dublin was solely a brewer of porter-style beer. "Plain Porter" was the drink of choice among the Irish working-class. Guinness later invented an unusually dark porter they called extra stout. Porters also followed English imperialism to India, China, and the Americas.

In those days, there was no such thing as chocolate or black malts that give today's porter its dark reddish-brown color. All that changed in 1817 with the invention of a drum-style malt roaster: The face of beer was forever changed.

Porter reached the height of its popularity in the mid-1800s. At that time advanced brewing and malting techniques allowed the widespread production of pale lager styles like pilsner, which consequently swept across Europe and America. Porter faded into history in England between the world wars. The last porter brewery in Ireland closed in 1973.

During the Great Beer Revival of the 1980s, porter rose phoenixlike from the ashes of history to take over, and maybe temporarily conquer, the microbrew revolution. First revived in London, where it all began, today there are scores of porters to chose from. Just about every microbrewery or brewpub brews a porter-style beer. It's the toast of home brewers and the favorite of a devoted cult of beer enthusiasts who can only stand beer that's the color of cola.

BEER NUMBER

8

Aventinus Wheat-Doppelbock
G. Schneider & Sohn
Kelheim, Bavaria, Germany

Platinum Medal: World Beer Championship, 1995

The Georg Schneider brewery in Kelheim is the world's oldest wheat beer brewery. It began production in the heart of Bavaria in 1607. Who can argue with that? You won't find a weiss beer this complex and delicious anywhere else on the planet. Aventinus is the world's oldest top-fermenting wheat doppelbock, bottle conditioned using the méthode champenoise with fresh yeast sediment on the bottom of the bottle. It's unfiltered, unpasteurized, double-fermented and made from pale, crystal, dark, and wheat malts.

This beer is deeply satisfying. Soft, round, rich and well blended. A wheat dopplebock this side of the Atlantic is a rare and unusual treat, and this beer's been imported to the United States only since 1994.

Aventinus has a big, rocky, tawny head. The expected clovelike taste of a wheat beer is mouthwatering, not cloying as in lesser offerings. Halfway through the beer, a scrumptious taste of smoked duck reveals itself. The yeast culture—possibly four centuries old—must have picked up many a savory smoked food fragrance from the air around the brewery. (German brewers have the talent to *isolate* some of the tastiest flavor profiles in their beer.) Aventinus reeks of the royal banquet. This beer has passed the flavor of a king's table to us, almost 400 years later—smoky, rich, delectable, slightly salty, well lagered, and nutty. There are few other beers that can boast such a highborn lineage and imperial palate.

BEERSTORY   The label is royal purple—and with good reason. The Schneider brewery is one of the thirty original Royal Court Breweries that were scattered throughout Bavaria and owned by the royal family Wittelsbach. In the 1850s, when wheat beer was declining in sales, the royal family leased several of their breweries to Georg Schneider. Today, the sixth generation of Georg Schneiders runs the brewery in Kelheim in the Danube River Valley.

Once upon a time, wheat beer was a drink only of the aristocracy. Indeed, Duke Maximillian I decreed in 1602 that the beer must not be brewed for public sale. By the mid-nineteenth century, however, only Georg Schneider was interested in brewing wheat beer. Golden pilsners had invaded from the east (Bohemia), and it seemed only little old ladies still drank wheat beers. In 1928, Schneider acquired the old Weissbraeuhaus in Kelheim that was considered the finest weizen brewery in the seventeenth and eighteenth centuries. Aventinus was created in 1907. Today the brew accounts for twenty-five percent of all beer sales in Bavaria.

Aventinus is imported to the United States by B. United International, an importer that was established in 1994 to bring the world's most distinctive beers to the United States. B. United imports several beers that are included in this book.

FOOD RECOMMENDATIONS   Aventinus is another beer that could be enjoyed straight from the glass. Also a perfect accompaniment to your own royal table. Serve with gourmet food such as roasted duck, pâtés and terrines, fruit, sharp cheeses, berries, and rich desserts.

RECOMMENDED RELATED BEERS   I recommend Schneider Weiss, another beer brewed by G. Schneider & Sohn. It is made with 60 percent wheat, and it's delicious.

SPECIFICATIONS   I paid $2.99 for a 16.9 oz. (500 ml) bottle of Aventinus. This beer is 7.7 percent alcohol by weight—warming and cozy. Aventinus is brewed by Privatbrauerei G Schneider & Sohn, 1-5 Emil Ott Strasse, 8420 Kelheim, Bavaria, Germany. Telephone: (09441) 7050. It is imported by B. United International, 75 North Central Avenue, Elmsford, NY 10523. Telephone: 914-345-8900. E-mail: 735-5053@mcimail.com.

BACKGROUND: A WHEAT BEER PRIMER

Wheat beers are considered to be the most thirst quenching of any beer. Brewed with 30 to 50 percent wheat in addition to barley, wheat beers come in many styles, from the light refreshing Berliner Weisse to the rich, clovelike weizenbiers made by many North American microbreweries. Berliner weisse style beer is lightly hopped and mildly alcoholic with a cloudy lactose-induced foam. Weizenbier is even wheatier with a higher alcohol content and full flavor. Wheat beer with yeast in the bottle is called *hefe-weizen*. Dark weizenbiers with malty body and fruity palate are called *dunkel* (dark) *weizen*. The alcoholic content of each wheat beer is listed below with its style. The wheat beers in this book are Aventinus Wheat-Doppelbock and Erdinger Pinkantus Weizenbock.

Wheat has been used for the brewing of beer since before the time of Tut. Actually, it was the Babylonians who first used a barley-wheat mixture to make their brews. The Egyptians had a cornucopia of wheat beers. Ancient Greek and Roman scribes tell of the Iberian Celts, who made a beer of wheat and honey called Corma. The Celts enjoyed the beer by sitting in a large circle and ordering slaves to carry a giant cup from one Celt to another. (There is no historical mention of Instant Corma.)

In medieval England occasional wheat shortages caused laws to be passed that prohibited brewers from brewing with wheat. Apparently some royal meddler did not believe that man lives by wheat beer alone. By the sixteenth century, wheat beer was a firmly established regional specialty in Bavaria. Even the famous Reinheitsgebot law—specifying that beer be made only from barley, hops, and water—had a loophole allowing Bavarian brewers to make wheat beer. By 1517, some German towns had two separate brewers guilds, the Weissbrauers (white, or wheat, brewers) and the Rothbrauers (red, or barley, brewers).

When millions of German immigrants came to America following the Civil War, they brought their wheat beers with them. Unfortunately, Prohibition destroyed the market in America, and by the time that "noble experiment" ended, many American beer drinkers had never even heard of wheat beer. The postwar U.S. brewers were not about to upset their barley-pop monopoly by introducing anything so unique and different as wheat beer to the general public. Leave it to the revolutionary microbrewers of the late twentieth century to reintroduce us to a style that's over six thousand years old.

In the past few years, beer made with wheat and barley has made a roaring comeback on the American scene. Even a few of the megabreweries have introduced wheat beers recently. And in a country full of pasta lovers why not? But the roots of the current wheat beer craze are planted deep in the German tradition. Perhaps a little lesson in wheat beer styles is in order, *mein herr und meine frau.*

The term wheat beer—or *weizenbier*—is somewhat generic. There are a dizzying array of wheat beers—and as many different spellings and (mis)pronunciations. Combine that with a wheat beer named *weisse,* which means "white," and you have further confusion because *weisse* and *weizen* are used interchangeably.

Weizenbier   The most common German wheat beer, from southern Germany and Bavaria, is called, technically, Suddeutsch weizen, or simply weizenbier. As tempting and fun as it is to say "wheezin' beer," it's pronounced something to the effect of "VITE-sen beer." No matter what you call it or how you say it, weizenbier has a clovelike bouquet and is sometimes served with a slice of lemon. Weizen is a crisp, fruity, tart drink with a low hop rate, light in body, and easy on alcohol. Once you've had one, there's no mistaking that flavor for any other style. Wheat beers are still extremely popular in Bavaria, accounting for twenty-five percent of all

beer sold there—and they drink a lot of beer. Weizens are 4.5 to 5.5 percent alcohol by volume. Carbonation levels are very high, and the head
might be as thick as meringue.

Hundreds of small German breweries produce weizenbiers, each with
its own special character. Most are forty to sixty percent malted wheat.
The top-fermenting yeast used in weizen releases a natural-occurring phe-
nolic compound that gives the beer its clove aroma. Another dose of yeast,
usually bottom fermenting, is added when bottling, giving the weizen a
cloudy look upon decanting. Weizen bottled with yeast usually says "hefe-
weizen" on the label—*hefe* being the German word for "yeast." Hefe-
weizens are sweet, soft, mild, and usually lack the clove flavor of filtered
weizen.

Kristall Weizen   *Kristall weizen* is (you guessed it) sparkling crystal in
appearance. Kristall weizen is weizenbier that has been filtered. Very pale
malts and long boils give kristall its clarity and stability. This stuff is the
equivalent of wheat champagne.

Berliner Weisse   The lightest wheat beer is called Berliner *weisse* (pronounced "vise" and sometimes spelled weiss). Berliner weisse is light in
body and alcohol and milky white in color. As the name implies, Berliner
weisse originated in the city of Berlin where it is served on hot afternoons.
It is sometimes poetically called the *kuhle blonde*, or "cool blond" of Berlin.

Berliner weisse is traditionally served in a bowllike goblet and hit with
a shot of woodruff or raspberry-flavored syrup. This gives the drink a dis-
concerting green (woodruff) or red (raspberry) color. The syrup offsets the
naturally sour flavor that is characteristic of the style.

Berliner weisse is probably the lightest and most refreshing of any
beer. It has a citrus palate and quenching finish that makes it a sum-
mertime treat. Berliner weisse goes great with cheese because, in a sense,
it is a dairy beer. Lactobacillus yeast is added to the beer in the secondary fermentation. That's a strain of the same type of yeast used in
yogurt. The bacillus in Berliner is specifically isolated for use in beer
only. It gives the beer a sour acidic bite, a milky cloudiness, and thick
white head. The lemonadelike cool blond of Berlin is 3 to 4 percent
alcohol by volume.

True aficionados of weisse pour $\frac{7}{8}$ of the bottle into a glass, then roll
the bottle on its side to make sure the cake of yeast on the bottom of the
bottle is completely suspended in the liquid. Then they pour the rich
whip-creamy foam on top of the already luscious head in the glass.

Believe it or not, the sour, lactose-laden weisse was the most popular wheat style in America before Prohibition. Almost every brewery made one, and it was served unfiltered and cloudy.

Dunkles Weissbier   To further mangle the language, another traditional German offering is *dunkles weissbier*, or literally, "dark white beer." Dunkel is a medium-bodied wheat beer with a copper color. Lemon is *not* added to dunkel, as that would ruin the malty rich spicy flavor. For further confusion, realize that dunkel—singular—ends in *-el*, but dunkles—plural—ends in *-les* That must be a result of too many dunkles.

Weizenbock   The darkest wheat beer is *weizenbock*—a bock wheat style, and a colossus among beers. Even though it's as dark in color as a dunkel, the dark tint doesn't come from adding copper-colored malt but from having such a high concentration of lighter colored malts—sometimes two or three times more. Weizenbock is a full bodied deep copper beer that is strong, alcoholic, and warming. It is usually served in winter, spring, or fall. Weizenbock has very little nose, is complex in flavor, with a warming breadiness.

American Wheat Beer   Just as every German brewery has its own take on wheat beer, so do their American counterparts. There are wheats made with honey, wheats made with California-style ale yeast, wheats whose clove flavors have been removed, and even a wheat *wine*, a drunk-as-a-lord cousin of barley wine.

Wheat is a tricky style with all that bizarre foreign yeast and odd grain floating around the brewery. The clovelike piquancy and the sour lactic yeast could absolutely destroy any pale ale made on the same premises. It's a lot harder for a small brewery to mix in a wheat without causing some problems further down the line. But brewing is an art and a science, and thank goodness, many are up for the challenge.

Wheat beers have for centuries been associated with good health. The slurry of nutritious yeast in the bottle gives it a wholesome reputation. A weizen revival in Germany has been led by young people who consider the beer "green" (as in ecologically correct).

Wheat beers are best when fresh—they are light and do not keep well. They should be served cool—at about 45 degrees Fahrenheit. Weizens are traditionally served in large, vase-shaped glasses that leave plenty of room for the ample, frothy head. First wet the glass under some cool water to keep the head under control. If you want to throw in a slice of lemon, great. But make sure your knife is clean. Any grease will destroy the beautiful froth.

If your head isn't spinning enough from all this talk of weisse and weizen, the Belgians have an entirely different wheat beer tradition that may be found under the Belgian Beer Primer section.

BEER NUMBER

9

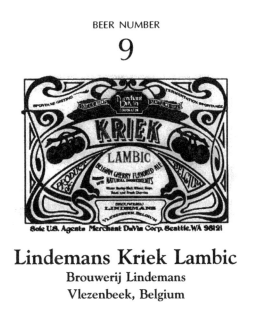

Lindemans Kriek Lambic
Brouwerij Lindemans
Vlezenbeek, Belgium

Best Wine: California's Summer Spectacular, 1994

You need a corkscrew to open this green bottle with red foil around the neck. This is a beer that I guarantee even a die-hard beer hater will love. After all, in a blind tasting at the California Summer Spectacular, Lindemans Kriek Lambic won a medal for Best Wine. Lindemans Kriek has a rosy-pink bubbly head and smells like cherry soda. As well it should—there's something like five pounds of cherries in every gallon of this lambic. Upon first sip, the sweet cherry bouquet is tempered by a tart wheat-oak flavor and a thick, smooth mouth feel. I can taste the green countryside in this beer. The beer does get a little cloying about halfway through, but at almost five dollars a bottle, you might just want to split it with someone special anyway. This is a great beer for Valentine's Day, Christmas, a birthday celebration, or any special occasion.

   Lindemans Kriek is produced at a Belgian farm brewery from a lambic base of 70 percent barley and 30 percent wheat. It is boiled with aged hops that have lost most of their bouquet but retain their bitterness. After a fermentation in which wild, airborne yeasts visit the beer, it is aged in oak barrels. Fresh cherries are added, creating a secondary fermentation.

BEERSTORY   Flemish master painter Peter Breugel pictured happy peasants dancing and drinking kriek in the seventeenth century. Lindemans began making kriek at their Belgian farmhouse brewery in 1811.

FOOD RECOMMENDATIONS   Pour this beer over ice cream! Drink it with roast duck made with cherries; turkey and cranberries; apricot-glazed country ham; crepes suzettes; cherries jubilee; crab and shrimp salad; and hors d'oeuvres. Serve cold in champagne glasses.

RECOMMENDED RELATED BEERS   Lindemans exports several fine lambics. I recommend their Framboise (raspberry lambic), Pêche (peach), Cuvée René, and Gueuze Lambic Grand Cru.

SPECIFICATIONS   The price is around $4.98 per 12 oz. bottle (355 ml). The alcoholic content of Kriek Lambic is about 5 percent by volume. Lindemans Kriek Lambic is brewed by Brouwerij Lindeman, 257 Lenniksebaan, 1712 Vlezenbeek, Belgium. Telephone: (02) 596 03 90. It is imported by Merchant du Vin, 140 Lakeside Avenue, Seattle, WA 98122-6538. Telephone: 206-322-5022. E-mail: info@mdv-beer.com.

BEER NUMBER

10

Murphy's Irish Stout
Lady's Well Brewery
Cork, Republic of Ireland

On my recent journey to Ireland I had ample opportunity to taste and compare all the great Irish stouts. Guinness may have invented the style, but I do believe Murphy's to be smoother, cleaner, and toastier than Guinness, which comes in a close second.

Murphy's is available in North America in pint cans graced with green hops and a heraldic shield on the label. The cans utilize the Draughtflow System, which makes it possible to savor the unique character of a cool Murphy's away from the pub. The Draughtflow cans contain an insert that releases a gas stream of nitrogen in fine bubbles as the can is opened.

The beer is infused with nitrogen and, when poured, looks different from beers one is used to seeing. It is frothy, tan, and creamy. Although it looks like head foam, it's actually nitrogen-infused stout. Taking a small taste is next to impossible, it's so smooth and refreshing you will find it hard not to drink half the glass in one gulp. Wow! There's a fine hop bitterness and roast coffee aftertaste. Murphy's is full bodied, smooth and easy to drink. It's no surprise that this relatively small brewery in Cork runs at full capacity seven days a week. This Irish stout is more than a tradition—it's a little bit of Celtic magic.

BEERSTORY   The Murphy brothers founded their brewery in 1856. They chose Cork's Lady's Well as a sight for the brewery because of its pure flowing spring water. The area surrounding Cork has naturally chalky soil which grows barley of the finest quality. The Murphy brothers converted an unused orphanage building into a brewery. The brewery occupies several city blocks in the middle of Cork's winding streets and twisting lanes. The original malt house was renovated in 1992, and today the beautiful antique structure has a steel and glass front and contains the brewery's offices. Kegs are stacked everywhere outside, and since most of Ireland's beer lovers do their drinking in the pub, the kegs are also piled up outside every bar. Flatbed trucks with kegs and tanks of nitrogen ply the narrow streets, bringing the black brew to Cork's thirsty drinkers.

Murphy's was purchased by Heineken in 1985 and since then they've gone international. A regional brand at home, Murphy's does a better percentage of their sales elsewhere around the world.

FOOD RECOMMENDATIONS   Murphy's Irish Stout is traditionally drunk with oysters. It also goes well with seafood, beef, corned beef, curry chicken, and traditional Irish foods as well as cold meats and cheese. It's good over vanilla ice cream (try it!) and excellent for picnics in the countryside, where faeries and druids might be lurking.

RECOMMENDED RELATED BEERS   Murphy's recently introduced their great stout in a bottle with a nitrogen widget so you can get the same great creamy brew out of a bottle. They've also introduced an Irish Amber which I highly recommend.

SPECIFICATIONS   I buy Murphy's Irish Stout for about $1.49 for a 14.9 oz. (440 ml) can. The alcoholic content is 3.4 percent by weight, 4.2 percent by volume. Murphy's is brewed at the Lady's Well Brewery, Leitrim Street, Cork, Republic of Ireland. Telephone: (021) 503371. It is imported by Heineken USA Inc., 50 Main Street, White Plains, NY 10606. Telephone: 914-681-4100.

Beers
Eleven Through Twenty

BEER NUMBER

11

Chimay Peres Trappistes
Abbaye de Notre-Dame de Scourmont
Chimay Abbey, Belgium

If you're looking for purity, wholesomeness, and brewing integrity, who better to trust than an abbey full of monks? Each bottle of Chimay is a work of art, worthy of careful study and prolonged delight.

Pronounced "SHE-may" this excellent beer's name has caused many a wit to yuck it up at the celibate Trappist brother's expense.

Chimay is copper-russet in color, with plenty of yeast bouquet. I recommend that you wet down the insides of your glass with water before pouring. Chimay veritably explodes out of the bottle with an outrageously billowing tan head. The foam is the reward for bottle conditioning but requires a patience I don't have—waiting for the head to settle. I always end up with a foamy nose when enjoying Chimay.

The earthy-yeasty-hoppy odor reeks of hidden cloisters, fresh soil, and ancient tomes. The bouquet can take you back two hundred years. Further study of the scent exposes apple blossoms and plums. The first sip reveals a beguiling smoky complexity that is in all-too-short supply in most of today's beers. I swear I can taste juniper in this beer, although it's not one of the ingredients. Chimay packs a 7 percent alcohol wallop that is practically hidden under its velvet texture.

The Trappist brothers take their brewing responsibilities as seriously as they take everything else. The water from the Artesian wells under the abbey are as close to perfection as any brewing water in the world. Absolutely nothing is added to the water and nothing is filtered out. The barley is grown without pesticides, and the malt is sprouted and kilned without chemical techniques. Hops are grown in the Hallertau region of Bavaria.

The beer is manufactured using the méthode champenoise. This process produces secondary fermentation right in the bottle that must be reined in with a cork and wire cap, just like champagne. This formula contributes to Chimay's unusual depth of flavor and allows it to be bottle aged. You can keep Chimay in your cellar for six months to a year.

BEERSTORY   The devoutly religious Trappist brothers established the Chimay Monastery in 1850. They began production of beer in 1863, insisting on all natural production, following the ancient monastic traditions in the art of brewing. Between World Wars I and II, Chimay popularized the term *Trappist beer*. In 1944, after the ravages of World War II, the monks repaired and renewed their brewery using the most advanced scientific methods available. They produced their first beer in the new brewery for the Easter celebration of 1948.

FOOD RECOMMENDATIONS   I would not share a beer this fine (and pricey) with anything so mundane as food. If pressed, I'd recommend apples, strawberries, and light cheeses on a blanket under a tree on a sunny day. Chimay is traditionally served in Belgium with a vinegary, peppery fish dish called *escavèche*. The Belgians also enjoy Chimay with the local game—rabbit, wild boar, and hare.

Sip it like a fine port, split it with a special friend, celebrate special occasions, or make any day a special occasion with this outstanding beer. Serve at 59 to 64 degrees Fahrenheit.

RECOMMENDED RELATED BEERS   Chimay produces three regular beers— all are excellent, well worth the price, and a must-try for any beer lover. The original, reviewed here, is the red cap, or *capsule rouge*, as the French say. The other Chimay beers are the white cap, or *capsule blanche*, bottled as Cinq Cents to mark the 500th anniversary of the town of Chimay in 1986. The strongest Chimay ale is the blue cap, or *capsule bleue*. It is 7 percent alcohol by weight, 9 percent by volume. This beer is closer to wine and may be aged five to ten years.

SPECIFICATIONS   Chimay is expensive. I have paid $3.29 for one 11.8 oz. (355 ml) bottle, and over $8 for a 25.3 oz. (750 ml) bottle. But considering it's one of the best beers in the world, and almost as alcoholic as wine, it is easily a bargain when compared to wine. The alcoholic content of Chimay Red Cap is 5.5 percent by weight, 7 percent by volume. Chimay is brewed at the Abbaye de Notre-Dame de Scourmont, 6483 Forges, Belgium. Telephone: (060) 21 0311. It is imported by Manneken-Brussel Imports, 1602 E. Cesar Chavez Street, Austin, TX 78702. Telephone: 512-472-1012.

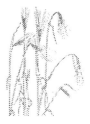

BEER NUMBER

12

Grant's Scottish Ale
Yakima Brewing and Malting Company
Yakima, Washington

Grant's Scottish Ale is one of my favorite beers for day-to-day drinking. It's honey-amber in color with the thick, chewy head that is so desirable in a Scotch ale. But like Grant's other beers, this one is beyond the style and, in my opinion, improved. It's like a ninety-shilling cask-conditioned ale of Scotland but with a big bouquet of Northwest Cascade hops that are added lavishly during the kettle boil. The aroma is sweet and caramel along with a flowery hop pungency. A fabulously full-tasting beer that is balanced, sweet, dry, and filling.

BEERSTORY   This was the first beer Bert Grant brewed when he opened his brewpub. Grant was born in Dundee, Scotland, and moved to Canada when he was two years old.

   Almost all of the hops grown in North America are grown in the Yakima River valley in Washington State. Bert Grant, owner of Yakima Brewing has been in the brewing business for more than fifty years. When he opened his brewpub in 1982, it was the first in the United States since Prohibition. His brewery was opened recently about three miles down from the brewpub. Worth a visit.

FOOD RECOMMENDATIONS   Drink with the flavors of the Pacific Northwest—salmon, river trout, fresh vegetables, shellfish, and herb-laden stews.

RECOMMENDED RELATED BEERS   Grant's makes a great line of beers. I recommend their Imperial Stout, Grant's IPA, Grant's Weis, and Grant's Celtic Ale.

SPECIFICATIONS   I pay about $7.99 for a six-pack of 12 oz. (355 ml) bottles of Grant's Scottish Ale. The alcoholic content is 4.7 percent by volume. Grant's Scottish Ale is brewed by Yakima Brewing and Malting Co., 1803 Presson Place, Yakima, WA 98902. Telephone: 509-575-1900.

BACKGROUND: A SCOTCH ALE PRIMER

Scotch ale is traditionally brewed in Scotland, where a hardy ale is necessary to help fend off the cold, wind, and rain. Scotch ale is strong, dark, and creamy. It's rich and chewy with a sweet malty character and a low hop bite. Today Scotch-style ales are also produced in Belgium, France, the United States, and Canada. Scotch ales weigh in at about 7 percent alcohol by volume. The Scotch ales listed in this book are Grant's Scotch Ale and MacAndrew's Scotch Ale.

Most people think of whisky when they hear "Scotch." But Scotland, which has the world's largest whisky distilling industry, is also known for praiseworthy beer styles.

Beer has been brewed in Edinburgh, Scotland, since monks began the practice there in the twelfth century. In days of old, the Scots brewed with heather, which sometimes contained hallucinogenic ergot fungus between its flowers. Home brewers there still make heather ale.

Scotch ale was a major export when the British Empire ruled the world, and Edinburgh was one of Europe's great brewing centers. As happened everywhere else, dozens of breweries closed down in Edinburgh in the late twentieth century. But today there are still a few excellent Scotch breweries left.

In a country where the only thing standing between you and the blistering north wind is a rock wall, a fireplace, and a beer, you'd better take your ale seriously. That is where the Scottish tradition of full-bodied, malty, strong ales originated. And the beers are fermented less completely than they might be, giving them a chewy, bold sweet-malt palate.

Scotch ales come in different strengths and are noted by their numbers, which harken back to the days of the shilling—a defunct denomination of British currency. The lightest Scotch ale is comparable to an English mild and is called "sixty-shilling" ale. The ale is actually dark in color but light in alcohol.

The ales get more expensive as they get stronger. A "seventy-shilling" ale is comparable to an English pale ale in strength and is also called a "heavy." An "eighty-shilling" ale is like an English bitter and is also called Export. A "ninety-shilling" ale is like an old ale or barley wine and is called a "wee heavy," especially if it is sold in small seven-ounce "nip" bottles. These numbers are said to have represented the price of a barrel of beer or the tax on a barrel.

Scotch ales are the perfect accompaniment to a hearty dinner, when one needs a little of the "wee heavy" to drive off the chill.

BEER NUMBER

13

IMPORTED BY PHOENIX IMPORTS, LTD., BALTIMORE, MD

Corsendonk Monk's Pale Ale
Brewery Corsendonk, Ltd.
Oud-Turnhut, Belgium

This is a pale ale, Belgian style. Corsendonk Monk's Pale Ale is brewed to the potent Belgian triple strength, and this beer is triple delicious. Lots of creamy yeast floating on the bottom of the bottle. It's cloudy gold in color with a cumulonimbus head of fluffy foam. There's an antique odor so characteristic of Monk's beer, but it's light. Do I taste morel mushrooms in butter? Dry and alcoholic up front. Warming. Yum! My blood pressure went down after the second sip. Clovey on the back of the tongue, tart and crisp. Clean and dry with a light citrus tang that jumps out of nowhere about halfway through the glass.

Corsendonk Monk's Pale Ale is brewed with all natural ingredients including 93 percent Plaisant and Triumph barley malts and 7 percent wheat. It's got four kinds of hops: Styrian Goldings, Hallertau, Herzbrucker, and Kent Challenger. This beer is bottle conditioned and can be cellared like fine wine to mature in the bottle. Cellaring gives Corsendonk the finesse of brut champagne—it becomes drier as it matures.

Corsendonk is imported by Phoenix Importers, a company that imports several of the premier beers in this book. Owner George Saxon is a gentleman, a gourmet, a beer writer, and all-round enthusiastic supporter of fine beers.

BEERSTORY   Corsendonk Abbey in Oud-Turnhout, Belgium, was funded through the munificence of Maria van Gelre, youngest daughter of Jan III, Duke of Brabant. In 1400 the monks of Corsendonk started a brewery which flourished until 1784, when the abbey was closed by Austrian ruler Jozef II.

In 1906, Antonius Keersmaekers founded a secular brewery nearby to revive the monks' brewing traditions. Antonius's grandson Jef continues the family tradition by brewing the Trappist-style Corsendonk to honor the monk's heritage.

FOOD RECOMMENDATIONS   This beer can be enjoyed before and after meals or with fish, fowl, seafood, and pasta. It goes well with the traditional Belgian mussels and fries. Also great with peppery food, dense cheese, pepper-smoked salmon, and spicy shrimp cocktail. Serve at 55 to 60 degrees Fahrenheit.

RECOMMENDED RELATED BEERS   Corsendonk also makes a Monk's Brown Ale that is a burgundy-colored ale with a fruity, smoky bouquet.

SPECIFICATIONS   Expect to pay up to $4 for a 12 oz. bottle (355 ml) of Corsendonk Monk's Pale Ale. It has a shelf life of up to 3 years. Alcoholic content is 6.11 percent by weight, 7.76 percent by volume. Corsendonk is brewed by Brewery DuBocq, for Brewery Corsendonk, Ltd., Oud-Turn-hut, Belgium. It's imported by Phoenix Imports, Ltd., 2925 Montclair Drive, Ellicott City, Baltimore, MD 21043. Telephone: 800-700-4ALE.

BEER NUMBER

14

Erdinger Pinkantus Weizenbock
Erdinger Weissbraü
Erding, Bavaria, Germany

The brewery of Erdinger Weissbraü brews a beer by the same name that is the largest-selling wheat beer in Germany—and in the world. They also brew the wonderful Erdinger Pinkantus Weizenbock. Erdinger specializes in weissbraü and, in fact, makes nothing but. These folks know how to brew with wheat.

Pinkantus is a top-fermented beer that is the specialty of the Erdinger brewery. It's strong, spicy, and smooth. The beer is bottle conditioned, which gives it a freshness that is startling. Pinkantus is low in hops and high in CO_2, which gives it a sweet palatability.

Pinkantus is brewed utilizing the brewery's own spring water. To quote the company's brochure: "It goes without saying that Erdinger Weissbraü produces its beer in accordance with the regulations on purity that go back to 1516."

BEERSTORY   The quaint town of Erding in Bavaria is at least fifteen hundred years old. There are timbered buildings and onion-domed church
towers in addition to two breweries. There were nine breweries in Erding
before World War II. The original Erding brewery dates from 1537 and is
today the sight of a pub. Erdinger Weissbräu was founded in 1886. It was
bought by Franz Brombach in 1935. Erdinger rose to the top of the
German wheat beer market in 1957. In 1983 the company built a new
brewery on the outskirts of Erding, near Munich. Today, Werner Brombach, son of the founder, runs the brewery.

FOOD RECOMMENDATIONS   Pinkantus can be enjoyed with such traditional
German foods as sausage, cheese, dumplings, chicken, and game.

RECOMMENDED RELATED BEERS   The brewery Erdinger Weissbräu makes
two other excellent wheat beers, Erdinger Weissbier Hefetrüb (with yeast)
and Erdinger Weissbier Kristallklar (without yeast).

SPECIFICATIONS   I paid about $2.99 for a 16.9 oz. (500 ml) bottle of
Erdinger Pinkantus. The alcoholic content of Pinkantus Weizenbier is 5.8
percent by weight, 7.3 percent by volume. Pinkantus Weizenbier is brewed
by Erdinger Weissbräu, 1-20 Franz Brombach Strasse, 8058 Erding,
Bavaria, Germany. Telephone: (08122) 4090. It is imported by Shamrock
Imports, 6550 East Washington Boulevard, City of Commerce, CA 90040.
Telephone: 213-724-1700.

BEER NUMBER

15

Guinness Stout
Arthur Guinness & Son
Dublin, Republic of Ireland

*The stout was of superior quality, soft against the tongue,
but sharp upon the orifice of the throat, softly efficient in its
magical circulation through the conduits of the body.*
—FLANN O'BRIAN, *AT SWIM TWO BIRDS*

Guinness Stout is the most popular stout in the world. And probably the first and only stout that many Americans encountered before the microbrewery revolution. Guinness's success has been so impressive that facts about the beer could go right in—well, the *Guinness Book of Records*, which was originally published by one of the brewing Guinnesses to settle arguments in pubs.

Okay, here goes: Guinness accounts for one in every two pints of beer sold in pubs in Ireland. It is exported to 130 countries. Guinness invented the stout style. Guinness advertising is so clever that it has won several industry awards. Guinness sponsors more sporting events and festivals in Ireland than any other company, including the Guinness Jazz Festival, the Galway Oyster Festival, the Wexford Festival Opera, the Temple Bar Blues Festival, the Rose of Tralee, and the Galway Races. Get the picture? Oh, and one more award. From me. Guinness is far and away the biggest, most global brewery to be included in this book. Their success has been based on their refusal to compromise quality for massive sales, and a pint of Guinness is still probably the best beer you can buy in most mainstream bars in America (if you're lucky).

There are two types of Guinness available at your bottle shop. The traditional bottle and the pint can, which is called Draught Guinness and contains a nitrogen packet. Nitrogen is less acidic than the usual CO_2, and this gives canned Draught Guinness a soft, sensuous, creamy foam that is not possible with CO_2.

Guinness has a majestic thick tan head and black body. It has a rich mix of roasted barley and a slight caramel flavor that is balanced perfectly by the hops. It's dry and refreshing.

BEERSTORY   Richard Guinness was a land agent to a rector in Celbridge, Ireland. He brewed beer for the rector's table. When the rector died, he left one hundred pounds to Richard's son Arthur Guinness, who was thirty-four years old. In 1759, Arthur took over an abandoned brewery at St. James's Gate in Dublin. In a move that will live forever in the annals of great deals, Guinness leased the brewery for nine *thousand* years at an annual rent of forty-five pounds. (I'll bet that rent is really going to skyrocket in the year 10,759.) At that time commercial beer production was virtually unheard of in Ireland. Most people drank whisky, gin, and a bootleg whisky called poteen. Guinness recognized a goldmine when he saw one.

Arthur started brewing ale mashed with a new type of malt imported from England. Called roasted barley, it gave Guinness beer a characteristically dark color and roasted toasty taste. As mentioned earlier, the beer was called porter because of its popularity with the porters of Covent Garden and Billingsgate in London, where porter brewing began in 1720. Guinness's porter ousted every import beer from the Irish market and took over part of the English market as well.

In the 1820s, Guinness produced a stronger porter called Extra Stout, and the rest—as they say—is beerstory. In time the name was shortened to Stout, and as the company brochure says: ". . . ultimately Stout and the family name of Guinness became nouns in their own right."

Becoming a noun paid handsome dividends. By 1833 the St. James's Gate brewery was the largest in Ireland. By 1881 Guinness was producing a million barrels of stout a year. By 1914 the brewery was the largest in the world. Though its sheer size has been surpassed by others, Guinness is still the biggest stout brewery in the world.

In the late 1980s, Guinness revolutionized brewing once again when it introduced the Draught Guinness in a can. But this ain't any can. The stout is sold in something called the In-Can-System. Basically, there is a plastic widget in the bottom of the can with a minute hole in it. The widget is filled with nitrogen. When the can is chilled, about one percent of the beer is forced into the hole. When the pressure is released, the nitrogen shoots into the beer. The nitrogen is less acidic than the usual CO_2 found in beer, and a can of Draught Guinness poured into a glass is a beauty to behold (and to be drinkin').

Guinness is huge. The brewery sprawls through a hundred acres of crowded, busy Dublin. The shipping yard is a pandemonium of forklifts, lorries, and machinery that was probably invented for the sole purpose of moving Guinness kegs. Security is tight. I guess they must mind their barrels. And who knows what the IRA could do if they got hold of all that stout.

The Hop Store is a shop with a cornucopia of Guinness souvenirs like nowhere else on Earth. There are green golf sweaters with the Guinness logo over the heart and Guinness socks, caps, T-shirts, flasks, and anything else a Guinness lover could want. One may even purchase Guinness underwear if one is so inclined. Tourists—some of them looking and acting suspiciously American—crowd around and take pictures for the folks back home. I too gave into the craving for a photo but was lucky enough to have my personal tour guide shoot it in front of the Guinness 500,000-pint mash tuns.

The actual brewery looks more like the control room at NASA than your typical bearded dude with a mash paddle in his hand. A huge board covers the wall with every pipe, switch, valve, and tank drawn in profile. Colored lights blink. "Brewers" sit behind gigantic, funky 1980s computer monitors and press a few waterproof buttons occasionally. From here they control every process in the brewery. They start brews, pick recipes, mash, lauter, and so on, without getting out of their Captain Kirk overstuffed control chairs.

I got a quick peek in the old brewery, which has been salvaged for every piece of recyclable metal. Consequently, it's a maze of old rusted stairwells, platforms, scaffolding, piping, cut wires, and the like. Guinness would love to sell the real estate—it's worth a fortune in the heart of downtown Dublin. But the buildings are historic, and so will be preserved.

The Guinness folks were rather coy about American Guinness and where it's made, but they have dozens of breweries all over the world, and you can bet your shillelagh that American Guinness ain't brewed in Ireland—except the pint cans of Draught Guinness with the nitrogen widget. They're definitely brewed in Ireland as there are only two canning plants in the world that can that stuff—one is in Ireland and the other in England, where Murphy's is canned. Guinness also makes Irish Budweiser, though at a different plant in Ireland.

FOOD RECOMMENDATIONS   Guinness Stout is dry, surprisingly low in calories (120), and wakes up the appetite. It has been drunk with every food imaginable. Particularly good with shellfish, seafood, and grilled meats. Oysters and stout are a famous marriage of food and drink in Ireland.

Guinness sent me a "Black List" that lists all the beverages people mix with distinctive Guinness Stout. Reluctantly, they had to admit that many of the mixtures were surprisingly pleasant. Others provoked mixed feelings. Here are a few of my favorites:

Guinness Velvet   A 50-50 mix of Guinness and champagne.

Top Hat   Popular in the 1930s, it's Guinness and ginger beer. Mixed to commemorate the dancing partners of Fred Astaire and Ginger Rogers.

Trojan Horse   Guinness mixed with cola. I recommend about two tablespoons of cola.

Guinness Shandy   Guinness and lemon-lime soda.

Tumbril   Guinness mixed with port wine, brandy, and champagne . . . in one glass!! Supposed to *cure* hangovers?! It's named after a *tumbril,* which is a cart used to carry condemned prisoners to the gallows. "You're only supposed to get into one if you feel like death." (*Note:* Author takes no responsibility for the effects of this one upon the reader.)

Red Head   Guinness and tomato juice (see above disclaimer).

Black & Black   Guinness and blackberry liqueur. (I saw quite a few people drinking this one in Dublin.)

Caribbean Cocktail   Believed to improve health, strength, and sex drive, this is drunk in the West Indies, mon. Mix Guinness with 3 oz. condensed milk, one raw egg, stir with nutmeg. Good luck!
    Wasp Sting   Guinness and orange juice. (Makes a lover-ly color.)
    Snake Bite   Guinness and cider.

And last but not least . . .
    Black & Tan   Guinness and Harp lager. The nitrogen in the Guinness keeps it afloat on top of the carbonated lager. To make at home, use canned Draught Guinness (which contains nitrogen) and pour it slowly over the back of a spoon.

SPECIFICATIONS   I've seen six-packs of Guinness in 12 oz. (355 ml) bottles on sale for $5.99. I've also seen it as high as $8.99. Canned Draught Guinness is about $1.69 for a pint can, about $5.99 for a four-pack. The alcoholic content of Guinness Stout sold in America is 4.8 percent by weight, 6 percent by volume. Draught Guinness is 3.4 percent by weight, 4.2 percent by volume. Guinness Stout is brewed by Arthur Guinness & Son, St. James's Gate, Dublin 8, Republic of Ireland. Telephone: (01) 453-6700. It is imported to the United States by Guinness Import Company, Six Landmark Square, Stamford, CT 06901-2704. Telephone: 203-359-7247.

BEER NUMBER

16

Orval
Abbaye de Notre-Dame d'Orval
Orval, Belgium

Orval is the quintessential Trappist ale. That's as it should be, for the brewing Benedictine Brothers inhabit the oldest established monastery among those that brew beer. The monastery was founded in the 1100s, although the modern Orval was not for sale until 1931.

Orval is deep orange in color. It has the sour-fruit bouquet typical of Trappist beers. The flavor has been described as "leathery." Orval has a firm body with a profound hop bitterness and a long, dry finish.

Orval is fermented three times with three kinds of malt and two kinds of hops that are grown to the brewery's specifications. The malts are Belgian and the hops are German and English. The beer is dry hopped, that is, hops are added to the secondary fermentation, not boiled. This gives Orval its hop kick. There are seven kinds of yeasts at work here, the final being added with candy sugar upon bottling. The beer is aged in the bottle for two months before it hits the market. Orval's flavor will improve if left upright in the cellar for up to five years.

BEERSTORY   The hamlet of Villers-devant-Orval is in the Belgian province of Luxembourg, in the valley of the Ardennes on the border of France.

The town is named "Golden Valley" in French, after a local legend which states that a countess from Tuscany lost a golden ring in a lake in the valley and pledged that if it were restored to her, she would thank God by building an abbey. The ring was brought to the surface by a trout, which today graces Orval's label and advertisements.

Orval also makes bread, a mild cheddar-style cheese, and a Trappist-style cheese resembling Port Salut.

FOOD RECOMMENDATIONS   Orval is drunk in Belgium as an aperitif. It is also enjoyed with semisoft mild cheese, warm brown bread, fresh pears, steamed mussels, clams in Pernod cream sauce, oysters, smoked salmon and trout, and calimari. Traditionally served in balloon glasses to capture the Belgian lace.

RECOMMENDED RELATED BEERS   The Brothers at Orval make only one beer, and they make it well. If you like Orval you might enjoy other Trappist beers such as Westmalle, La Trappe (from the Netherlands), Rochefort, and Chimay.

SPECIFICATIONS   Orval is a high-quality beer with a rather high price. At $3.29 for an 11.2 oz. bottle (330 ml), you are getting one of the best beers in the world aged to perfection. This vintage-dated chardonnay of the beer world may be cellared for years. Alcoholic content of Orval is 5.4 percent by weight, 6.48 percent by volume. Orval is brewed by Trappist monks at Abbaye de Notre-Dame d'Orval, 6823 Villers-devant-Orval, Belgium. Telephone: (061) 31 10 60. Orval is imported by Merchant du Vin, 140 Lakeside Avenue, Seattle, WA 98122-6538. Telephone: 206-322-5022. E-mail: info@mdv-beer.com.

BEER NUMBER

17

Samuel Smith's Imperial Stout
Samuel Smith Old Brewery
Tadcaster, Yorkshire, England

Gold Medal: California Beer Festival, 1995

Imperial indeed! This style was invented to ship across the Baltic to the tsar. Samuel Smith's Imperial Stout is as royal purple as a beer can be. It's rich and complex with a roast barley and perfume hop nose. Chocolate cake in a bottle. This is a beer to be savored. Every sniff and every sip is concentrated ecstasy. I never understood the motivation to be a tyrant tsar of Russia until I realized that the reward was Imperial Stout. Worth a coup d'état or two.

BEERSTORY   Another great offering from Samuel Smith Old Brewery in Tadcaster. This style was revived by the brewery in 1980 at the request of their American importer, Charles Finkel. Imperial Stout was first shipped to Catherine the Great, queen of all the Russias, who requested a beer that was powerful, with lots of malt and hops. So great was Catherine's thirst for strong stout that Imperial Russia quickly became England's biggest export customer.

Samuel Smith's Imperial Stout is the crown jewel in a great line of beers, each brewed in square slate fermenters called Yorkshire Squares. As the company literature puts it: "Samuel Smith's Imperial Stout reigns supreme. Crowned with a head of tiny bubbles like fine champagne, her robe is black velvet, with the nature of a benevolent queen—gentle, yet powerful." I couldn't have said it better. All hail, Catherine!

For more about the Samuel Smith Brewery see beer no. 7, Samuel Smith's Taddy Porter.

FOOD RECOMMENDATIONS   This beer is recommended for serving in a brandy snifter at 60 degrees Fahrenheit. Drink with Stilton cheese and walnuts, New York cheesecake (divine decadence!), steak au poivre, caviar, oysters Rockefeller, oysters casino, champagne, espresso, and Cuban cigars.

RECOMMENDED RELATED BEERS   Samuel Smith does not make a bad beer, and, in fact, most of their products are listed elsewhere in this book. I highly recommend the Famous Taddy Porter, Old Brewery Pale Ale, Nut Brown Ale, and Winter Welcome. These folks even make a great lager, Samuel Smith's Lager—a rarity in that part of the world.

SPECIFICATIONS   Imperially priced at $10.99 a six-pack, it's well worth the extra few bucks. This is, after all, the beer of queens and kings. The alcoholic content of Samuel Smith's Imperial Stout is 5.9 percent by weight, 7.6 percent by volume. It's brewed at The Old Brewery, Tadcaster, Yorkshire, LS24 9DSB, England. Telephone: (0937) 832 225. It is imported by Merchant du Vin, 140 Lakeside Avenue, Seattle, WA 98122-6538. Telephone: 206-322-5022. E-mail: info@mdv-beer.com.

18

Saison Dupont
Brasserie Dupont
Hainaut, Wallonia, Belgium

The saison style has been called the "most endangered species" among Belgian beer styles. And it's easy to see why. Beers in the saison style— like Saison Dupont—are Belgian farmhouse ales, made in artisanal brew- eries that more resemble museums than beer factories. Saison Dupont is the undisputed classic of this snappy, bright, yeasty style.

The cork pops off Saison Dupont like champagne. A pretty white cloud of foam comes out of the neck of the green bottle. I'm expecting a gusher, but it's just a polite blub patiently waiting for me to ready my glass, which I wet to cut down on the foaming. I pour ever so slowly because it's as frothy as can be. The dense white head is like a meringue. Once poured, the golden Dupont issues forth a lively tickle-your-nose bouquet. The champagne analogy continues—orange-lemony sour, herbal, tart, and clean, not acidic. There's that unmistakable, almost boysenberry, Belgian backthroat. My taste buds are singing happily as my belly warms with a satisfied glow.

The beer is made with an unruly, clumpy yeast that would be the bane of most breweries. The yeast was cultured for its taste and aromatic qual- ities and looks a little daunting floating around in the beer. But in spite of—actually because of—this weird yeast, you get a delicious, thirst-quenching ale with the fresh, wholesome character you'd expect from other farm-fresh products.

BEERSTORY   The Dupont brewery is located in Wallonia in the French-speaking part of Belgium and is run by Marc Rosier and his two sisters, who are third-generation Duponts. The brewery dates from 1850 and is a classic farmhouse brewery which has been in the Dupont family since 1920. Also a working farm, eggs are sold from the "executive" offices. The yeast was not bred to sit politely on the bottom of the bottle because Dupont was not brewed to travel. Until recently the farmhouse brewery sold only one beer, and you had to buy it at the brewery. Even in Belgium, Dupont does not deliver. If you want the beer you have to come get it.

FOOD RECOMMENDATIONS   Saison Dupont is dry, lemony, and very hoppy, making it a great match for oysters and other seafood. Also recommended with fowl, pâtés, and tarts made with onion and cheeses. This beer was originally made for farm workers and so makes a natural accompaniment to hearty, grainy bread, vegetables and salads, chicken, and sausage.

RECOMMENDED RELATED BEERS   The folks at Dupont are into sustainable agriculture and offer a new beer called Foret, which is the only certified organic saison beer in Belgium. Highly recommended.

SPECIFICATIONS   Like any fabulous, handmade piece of art, Saison Dupont is not inexpensive. I paid about $7.99 for a 25.4 oz. (750 ml) champagne-style bottle.
　　Dupont is smooth, delicious, and goes down exceedingly well, but it's deceptively potent. Alcoholic content is 7 percent by volume. Dupont is brewed at Brasserie Dupont, 5 Rue Basse, 7904 Tourpes-Leuze, Belgium. Telephone: (069) 66 22 01. It is imported by Vanberg & Dewulf, 52 Pioneer Street, Cooperstown, NY 13326. Telephone: 607-547-8184.

BEER NUMBER

19

Pinkus Ur-Pils (Organic)
Brauerei Pinkus Müller
Münster, Germany

There's something very appealing about organic beer. All sorts of ques-
tionable chemicals are used in the farming of barley and hops. Chemicals
are also used during the sprouting and germination of green malt. It's very
difficult to track down organic barley, and even more so organic hops.
But the trend today is toward organics in food, so why not in beer?

Organic is one thing, but it's still got to be good beer. And Pinkus Ur-
Pils is as golden as sunshine. There's a nice, even frosty head. At first
sniff, I register the organic hop from the Hallertau region, but they're
slightly overpowered by the malt. There's a back-of-the-throat sweetness
and a lingering tartness. As dry and well balanced as you'd expect from a
pilsner-style lager. About halfway through I sense the strangest thing—a
salty taste of smoked meat and Münster cheese. Well, this beer *is* from
Münster. . . . One more incidence of beer yeast being positively influenced
by the food yeasts floating around with it. The beer suddenly becomes a
sandwich—the bready maltiness mingling with the savory smoked-beef-
and-cheese palate. Wow! This is followed up by a sweet dessertlike aftertaste. Now that's a restorative! It reminds me that beer was first and
foremost the earliest transportable food product. When people couldn't

even get a meat and cheese sandwich, at least they had their beer to take its place. And it's organic.

BEERSTORY   Pinkus Müller makes the longest-standing organic beers sold in the United States. The brewery in Münster dates to 1816, when Johannes Müller opened a bakery and brewery. Not too long ago, Pinkus began to brew the organic Ur-Pils for a Dutch health food store. The brewery went completely organic when Barbara, the youngest daughter of the current generation of Müllers, completed her studies at Munich's Weihenstephan brewing school. Ms. Müller became the family's first female brewster.

FOOD RECOMMENDATIONS   The beer tastes like a good sandwich, so if follows that it goes great with a real sandwich—on dark, grainy bread with lettuce, tomatoes, onions, light meat, and cheese. Merchant du Vin, the importer, recommends that you enjoy Pinkus Ur-Pils with trout almandine, fresh salmon, hors d'oeuvres, quiche Lorraine, cobb salad, gazpacho, tabbouleh, garlic or shallot sauces, thick potato chips, fresh strawberries, and cherries.

The Pinkus Home Brew Haus, the brewery's brewpub, is famous for its Altbierbowle, a refreshing drink made by pouring Pinkus Altbier over seasonal fruit. Serve at 45 degrees Fahrenheit.

RECOMMENDED RELATED BEERS   Pinkus Müller makes two other great beers that are available in the United States—Pinkus Münster Alt and Pinkus Weizen. Both are high on my list of the world's best beers.

SPECIFICATIONS   Organics always cost a little more, but this beer is worth the expense. I pay about $2 for a 12 oz. (355 ml) bottle, and $10.99 for a six-pack of Ur-Pils. The alcoholic content of Ur-Pils is about 5 percent by volume. Pinkus Ur-Pils is brewed by Brauerei Pinkus Müller, 4-10 Kreuz Strasse, 4400 Münster, Nordrhein-Westfalen, Germany. Telephone: (0251) 45151-52. It is imported by Merchant du Vin, 140 Lakeside Avenue, Seattle, WA 98122-6538. Telephone: 206-322-5022. E-mail: info@mdv-beer.com.

BACKGROUND: A PILSNER PRIMER

Pilsner lager is by far the most popular beer style in the world. Dry, bubbly, and golden, good pilsners have a round malt character with a flowery hop aroma and well-balanced bitterness. The style orginated in Pilsen, Bohemia, now part of the Czech Republic. Real pilsner should not be confused with mass-produced American pilsners, which are brewed with corn or rice as adjuncts and have a barely discernible hop aroma or flavor. Several American craft breweries do, however, make world-class pilsners. Pilsner has an alcoholic content of approximately 5 percent by volume. The pilsners in this book are Pinkus Ur-Pils, Pilsner Urquell, Scrimshaw Pilsner Style Beer, and Dock Street Bohemian Pilsner.

Eighteen forty-two was a watershed year for beer. For the previous ten thousand years, all beer was dark and cloudy. But in the fifth decade of the nineteenth century a brand-new brewery in Pilsen, Bohemia, rolled out the world's first translucently golden lager beer. Other lagers had been made at the time, but none with the look of sparkling champagne. Of course, it was an instantaneous sensation in Europe's sidewalk cafes.

Like all great innovations, pilsner was immediately copied across the world—and the name was stolen too. Sometimes spelled pilsener or pils, the spelling wasn't the only thing that was corrupted. Today almost every bad beer in the world is some pitiful imitation of a pilsner-style lager. There are millions of people who are not even aware there *is* any other kind of beer.

The flowery hop bouquet of a real pilsner is provided by Saaz hops grown in Bohemia. These hops are exported to breweries in North America that brew true-to-style pilsners.

Pilsner means simply, "from Pilsen." The name was never trademarked, and like many other brand names, fell into general usage. By 1898, hundreds of golden lagers in Europe and abroad were called pilsner. The original brewery that invented the style renamed its product Pilsner Urquell, the second word meaning "original source." That is not a lightly made claim, and, indeed, there can be no argument that Pilsner Urquell is the definition of the style. Every other pilsner, whether great or small, is an imitation.

A brewer called Josef Grolle is credited with inventing pilsner-style lager. Grolle was employed by the owners of Pilsen's two brewpubs to create a beer that would compete with dark Bavarian lagers. The two brewpubs merged, and soon Grolle was experimenting with malting temperatures to malt a barley that would yield the unheard-of golden color.

Once done, Grolle had to experiment with mixing yeasts that would give the beer its desired clarity. Grolle's work paid off.

In the seventeenth and early eighteenth centuries, no one would have known or cared about such a light-colored beer. In those days, drinking vessels were leather, ceramic, or metal. With a thick mug, in the dim candlelight of the time, one wouldn't have noticed if one's beer was blue. When mass-produced clear glasses became available, a sparkling golden beer could be enjoyed for its visual merits. Fortunately, the taste was appealing as well—light and, oh, so modern.

The innovations in malting and scientifically controlled brewing that were a hallmark of pilsner soon spread across Europe along its new railway system. The railroads also allowed Pilsner Urquell to be easily transported to Prague, Vienna, and Berlin. Émigrés from those cities took the pilsner style to America, where, after the Civil War, they began opening breweries in New York, Pennsylvania, Cincinnati, Milwaukee, and St. Louis.

It is said that the farther one gets from the city of Pilsner, the less appealing the pilsner beer becomes. Germany—of course—makes some very good pilsners. The large breweries of Belgium produce some decent pilsners. The Netherlands gives us Heineken and Grolsch, two export-style pilsners. Heineken is probably the world's most famous "import" beer.

Most American microbreweries are ale breweries. The extra time and refrigeration needed for pilsners makes them less cost-effective in an already cash-strapped business. There are, however, some notable micro-brewed pilsners that can compete with Czech products—especially when it comes to freshness.

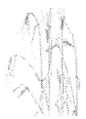

BEER NUMBER

20

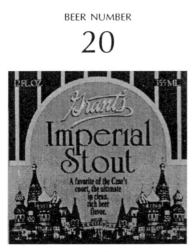

Grant's Imperial Stout
Yakima Brewing and Malting Company
Yakima, Washington

A favorite of this beer tsar's court, Grant's Imperial Stout is rich, clean, and smoky. This is stout times five. Once again, royalty enters into the flavor profile. I can discern roasted grouse, heather and honey, rose and gunpowder. Grant's delivers that rarefied air of the imperial court with enough gratifying food flavors in the palate to sustain any Russian king. Let me list the flavors: It tastes like crispy crackers, saltwater taffy, a caramel nougat, and is spicy-sweet—like a deep pine forest. It doesn't get much richer than this and still remain beer!

Grant's Imperial Stout is made with pale, crystal, and black malts. It's unusual in that it contains honey, which kicks the alcohol content up without adding too much of a cloying sugariness. The Russian Imperial Palace is on the red label. Too many of these and you'll be hootin' with Rasputin!

For more on Yakima Brewing Co., see Grant's Scottish Ale.

FOOD RECOMMENDATIONS   Savor with Cotswald cheese. Wash down smoked salmon. Or enjoy by itself, sipped from snifters.

RECOMMENDED RELATED BEERS   Grant's makes great beers. I recommend their Scottish Ale, Grant's IPA, Grant's Weis, and Grant's Celtic Ale.

SPECIFICATIONS   I pay about $7.99 for a six-pack of 12 oz. (355 ml) bottles of Grant's Imperial Stout. The alcoholic content is 6.2 percent by volume. Grant's Imperial Stout is brewed by Yakima Brewing and Malting Co., 1803 Presson Place, Yakima, WA 98902. Telephone: 509-575-1900.

5

Beers
Twenty-one Through Thirty

BEER NUMBER

21

Old Peculier
T&R Theakston
Masham, Yorkshire, England

Masham is an appropriately named town in Yorkshire, where an appropriately named ale called Old Peculier has been made since 1827. The name comes from the old Norman French word that means particular rather than odd, and it's spelled -er instead of -ar. And Old Peculier is indeed for the particular drinker.

Old Peculier is the old-ale-style classic. It's created from six different malts and several brewing sugars blended to produce a timeless taste. The ale is curranty and raisiny, with a chocolate nose. A deep whiff reveals fertile waves of barley on an English hillside on a hot summer's afternoon. Deep flavor, as of the fecund soil of Yorkshire. Old Peculier actually tastes as good as it smells—that's something that's highly unusual. It's fruity and complex with a vaguely burnt caramel palate and Fuggle hop bitterness. This is an ale I can enjoy again and again.

T&R Theakston employs a cooper, Clive Hollis, and his apprentice on site (they are one of the last breweries in the world to do so) and it's the cooper's job to build and repair the Polish oak barrels that Old Peculier is aged in. Using his eye and his skills, Hollis builds thirty-six-gallon, absolutely watertight, casks that last up to sixty years.

The barrels at Theakston must stand up to pressures of forty pounds per square inch. Empty, they weigh 140 to 160 pounds. The first time out, they are filled with mild beer to mellow the oak gently. The wood gives the beer a singular taste. History lives between the grains of the oak, along with unique yeasts and bacteria that flavor the beer. Stainless steel might be the best thing for building an automobile, but wood is the only way to properly store beer.

BEERSTORY   The Theakstons arrived in Mashamshire, in the fertile valley of the River Ure, during the time of the Viking raiders. Brewing was probably introduced to the area by monks around the same time.

Masham grew to a prosperous market town famous for its sheep sales. In 1827, Robert Theakston took the lease of the Black Bull pub and brewhouse in Masham. He was very successful, and by the 1840s he acquired many pubs in the area, all of which sold his popular ales brewed at the Black Bull Brewhouse.

Robert was joined by his two sons. The demand for Theakston's ale grew, but the brewhouse could no longer keep up with supply. A new brewhouse and maltings were built and opened in 1875. This brewery is still used by Theakston today. Little has changed except the belt drive to the grist mill is now powered by an electric motor instead of steam. And today, the copper brew kettle is heated by an oil-fired burner instead of an open furnace. The brewer says: "Our suppliers want this hop filter for their museum. We need it to make our beer."

Today the Theakston brewery is a popular tourist attraction, receiving over twenty thousand visitors a year.

FOOD RECOMMENDATIONS   A sweetish beer, Old Peculier goes well with densely flavored foods such as prime beef and hearty meat stews. Traditionally enjoyed with pickled herring and gingerbread made with oatmeal and molasses.

RECOMMENDED RELATED BEERS   Theakston makes an excellent bitter and an extra bitter that is available in Great Britain.

SPECIFICATIONS   I paid $1.99 for a single 12 oz. bottle (355 ml) of Old Peculier and about $10.99 a six-pack. Old Peculier has an alcoholic content of 4 percent by weight, 5.2 percent by volume. It is brewed by T & R Theakston, Wellgarth, Masham, Ripon, Yorkshire, HG4 4DX, England. Telephone: (0765) 689544. Old Peculier is imported by Scottish & Newcastle Importers Co., 444 De Haro, Suite 209, San Francisco, CA 94107. Telephone: 415-255-4555.

BACKGROUND: AN OLD ALE PRIMER

Old ales are rich, creamy, malty-sweet, and deep reddish-brown in color. They may possess a currant- or raisinlike flavor with a hint of molasses. This is achieved with the addition of brown or candy sugar, not fruits. The thickness of old ale suggests a high alcoholic strength that is sometimes—but not always—present. Old ales are about 5.6 to 7 percent alcohol by volume. The old ales listed in this book are Old Peculier, Third Coast Old Ale, and Thomas Hardy's Ale (Vintage 1994).

Folks always seem to think that things were better in the "old days." That may or may not be true. I think beer consumers today have a greater selection of fresh, quality-beer styles than at any other time in history. But still . . . many great beers envoke a sweet perfume of the past that is truly vitalizing. There's something special about savoring flavors that our great-great-grandmothers and -grandfathers enjoyed. Such is the romance with old ale.

But old ale can mean more than some vague nostalgia for the past. In fact, some old ales are actually old; they're aged like wine. And any ale expected to stand up to such aging must be strong, lest it become contaminated. That was especially true in the good old days.

Old ale is primarily an English style, although there are a few exquisite American-micro old ales. Some old ale may be classified as barley wine, which is even stronger. The brewers of old ale do not ferment it as completely as it might be. This is done on purpose to leave the sweetness and body of the malt sugars in the brew. This gives old ale a thick mouth feel and creamy consistency.

English brewers reserve some of their drollest names for old ales, including Old Peculier, Wobbly Bob, Old Buzzard, and Owd Roger. And lest we forget, the immortal Old Jock and Old Fart.

Some old ales were originally so-named because they were strong beers made in winter and meant to be laid down until summer when brewing was not possible. The name implies that the ale is months—or even years—old. This style of old ale may have been blended with younger ales before serving.

Old ale may be aged in a tank or in a bottle. Tank aging is usually from six to twelve months. Bottle aging is up to the consumer, but some old ales may be aged for six, seven, or even twenty years. Aging gives the old ale a port wine or brandylike flavor. Ale bottle aged with yeast may increase its alcohol content by two to five percentage points, from about 7 percent to 9 or 12 percent. Because of the vicissitudes of such a process, every batch of aged old ale will turn out different.

Aged old ales are naturally more expensive, since such quality does not come cheap. And even if the imbiber cannot afford to drink it regularly, it's surely worthy of a birthday or anniversary. Besides, the best bottle of beer only equals the cost of an average-quality bottle of wine. Old ales are rare and refined and represent the zenith of the brewer's art.

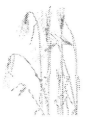

BEER NUMBER

22

Liefmans Frambozenbier
Brouwerij Liefmans
Oudenaarde, Belgium

Try saying "fram-BO-zen-BEER" a few times. Go ahead. It's fun. But not as much fun as drinking one. Most Belgian raspberry ales are lambics, usually made from gueuze-style beer. Not so Frambozenbier from the Liefmans brewery of Oudenaarde. It's made with a base of the world-famous Goudenband brown ale. First introduced in 1985, Liefmans Frambozenbier quickly came to be regarded as one of the country's classic raspberry beers.

Frambozenbier has a sweet and sour bouquet with a tan head. There's an almost biscuity flavor in the back of the throat. A bittersweet angel of a tart beer. Peerless. The tissue-wrapped bottle is adorned with a label festooned with dancing cupids holding gigantic raspberries high above their heads. The overtones of fresh raspberries mingle with the characteristically winelike flavor of Goudenband to produce a "symphony of palate and aroma that can't be matched."

Frambozenbier is made with whole raspberries and raspberry juice. It's bottled conditioned in champagne bottles and at least two years old before leaving the brewery. The bottling date is stamped on the cork.

BEERSTORY   The historic town of Oudenaarde is located in French East Flanders on the River Scheldt. The monk Arnold—the patron saint of brewers—was a brewer in Oudenaarde in the eleventh century. The Liefmans brewery has been brewing since at least 1679. The brewery was run, several centuries later, by a flamboyant ballet dancer named Madame Rose, whose picture used to grace every bottle. At the beginning of 1990, Ms. Rose retired and sold the brewery to the Riva Group of West Flanders.

FOOD RECOMMENDATIONS   Frambozenbier should be served at or just above cellar temperature. This pink champagne of the beer world is a perfect match for chicken, duck, and game birds. It's sinful with rich, dark chocolate and refreshingly restorative at any time. It can also be used to marinate meat to superb results. Serve this instead of champagne. Trick beer haters. They'll think it's the best thing they've ever drunk.

RECOMMENDED RELATED BEERS   If you can find a Liefmans Goudenband brown ale, you can taste the base of Frambozenbier. Liefmans also makes a kriek, which is a cherry beer in which seven pounds of Schaerbeeck cherries are added to each gallon of Goudenband beer.

SPECIFICATIONS   This is a pricey brew but worth it. Liefmans Frambozenbier is two years old when purchased and can be aged for two to three years. I pay from $5 to $7 per 12.7 oz. (375 ml) bottle.

Alcoholic content is 3.9 percent by weight, 5 percent by volume. Liefmans Frambozenbier is brewed at Brouwerij Liefmans, 200 Aalst Straat, 9700 Oudenaarde, Belgium. Telephone: (055) 31 13 92. It's imported by Phoenix Imports, Ltd., 2925 Montclair Drive, Ellicott City, Baltimore, MD 21043. Telephone: 800-700-4ALE.

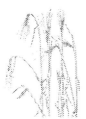

BEER NUMBER

23

Samuel Smith's Oatmeal Stout
Samuel Smith Old Brewery
Tadcaster, North Yorkshire, England

This beer is so dense I can just barely see light through it. It radiates a deep, hearthside warmth that I receive before even tasting it. I can smell the fruity ale yeast escaping into the air as the gentle tan head pushes it up through the malt. This stout is a treat! A complex, medium-dry palate, roasty, with a bittersweet aftertaste. Smooth as silk. The roast and chocolate malts finish surprisingly dry and long. The barley malts also give it a sharpness. I swear I caught hint of hot, gooey caramel buns on the second swig. The beer is as fortifying as an oatmeal drink can be. Well made and well worth the price.

BEERSTORY   Once upon a time, oatmeal stout was prescribed as a drink for nursing mothers and athletes. This dates from a time—around the turn of the nineteenth century—when nutritional stouts were in fashion. Oats are in the barley family and a small addition to beer yields a great flavor. Oatmeal stout was virtually extinct in 1980, when Samuel Smith began to brew the style for its American importer, Merchant du Vin of Seattle. Since that time, dozens of other breweries have begun to brew the style, both in England and microbrew America.

Samuel Smith's is an independent family-owned company and, established in 1758, the oldest brewery in Yorkshire. They brew their beer the old-fashioned way, using huge, slate stone fermenters called Yorkshire Squares. (For more on Samuel Smith's Brewery see beer no. 7, Samuel Smith's Taddy Porter.)

FOOD RECOMMENDATIONS   This beer goes great with English pub fare and seafood. Serve with steamed clams, grilled tuna, lobster with drawn butter, roast beef, steak and kidney pie, bangers and mash, ploughman's lunch, game, crumpets, dark bread, and Stilton cheese. Serve at 55 degrees Fahrenheit.

RECOMMENDED RELATED BEERS   Every single beer made at Samuel Smith's Old Brewery is a classic. I recommend Samuel Smith's Taddy Porter, Imperial Stout, Nut Brown Ale, Old Brewery Pale Ale, Winter Welcome Ale, and Pure Brewed Lager Beer.

SPECIFICATIONS   Samuel Smith's Oatmeal Stout is about $3 for a 18.2 oz (550 ml) bottle, about $9 for a six-pack of 12 oz. (355 ml) bottles. The alcoholic content is 3.6 percent by weight, 4.62 percent by volume. Samuel Smith's is brewed at The Old Brewery, Tadcaster, Yorkshire, LS24 9DSB, England. Telephone: (0937) 832 225. The beer is imported by Merchant du Vin, 140 Lakeside Avenue, Seattle, WA 98122-6538. Telephone: 206-322-5022. E-mail: info@mdv-beer.com.

BEER NUMBER

24

Royal Oak Pale Ale
Eldridge Pope
Dorchester, Dorset, England

The gorgeous amber-copper color of Royal Oak is as inviting as a crackling fireplace on a rainy autumn afternoon. A fine tawny head coats the
glass with a thick curtain of Belgian lace as it collapses into a rocky snowcap of foam. This ale is naturally fermented, and it has a fruity, dry nose
with a whiff of Goldings hops. The palate is complex and nutty with the
slightest hint of currants. Bitter on the back of the tongue, this is indeed
a royal ale.

Made by Eldridge Pope, this beer is brewed by traditional methods,
which depend on the skill and art of the brewers that have been handed
down from generation to generation—not on computer control panels.
This pale ale contains pale and crystal malts, whole-cone Fuggles and
Goldings hops, and a strain of top-fermenting yeast that has been in use
for generations.

BEERSTORY   The royal purple and gold label shows a picture of King
Charles II surrounded by oak leaves. This signifies the legend of Charles
II, who hid from Oliver Cromwell's soldiers in a great oak tree from dawn
until dusk on September 6, 1651. In King Charlie's own words: "We carried with us some victuals . . . bread, cheese, beer . . . and got up in a

great oak tree that had been lopped some three or four years before, being grown out again, very bushy and thick, could not be seen through . . . while we were there we could see soldiers going up and down in a thicket, searching for persons escaped."

Royal Oak is brewed by Eldridge Pope & Co. in Dorchester, a city that has been a brewing center since 1760. Eldridge Pope was started when Charles Eldridge and his wife, Sarah, took over the Antelope Hotel in 1833. The success of the venture led them to establish the Green Dragon Brewery in 1837. Pope died in 1846, and Sarah ran the brewery until 1870, when it was acquired by Edwin Pope and his brother Alfred. A new brewery was built in 1880 next to a railroad line, and Eldridge Pope served pubs up and down the line. The brewery burned down in 1922 but was rebuilt in its original style. Today the brewery owns nearly two hundred pubs and is run by Alfred Pope's grandson and three great-grandsons.

FOOD RECOMMENDATIONS   Delicious with roast beef, sirloin, lamb, such English foods as fish and chips, Huntsman cheese, and dark, crusty breads. Royal Oak should be served at 55 to 60 degrees Fahrenheit.

RECOMMENDED RELATED BEERS   Pope's 1880 Ale, Royal Oak Strong Ale, and Goldie Barley Wine are great beers made by Eldridge Pope, but I'm not aware that you can find them in the United States.

SPECIFICATIONS   I pay about $2 per 11.15 oz. (330 ml) bottle of Royal Oak, about $10.69 a six-pack. The alcoholic content of Royal Oak is 3.6 percent by weight, 4.8 percent by volume. Royal Oak is brewed by Eldridge, Pope & Co., Weymouth Avenue, Dorchester, Dorset, DT1 1QT, England. Telephone: (0305) 251251. Royal Oak is imported by Phoenix Imports, Ltd., 2925 Montclair Drive, Ellicot City, Baltimore, MD 21043. Telephone: 800-700-4ALE.

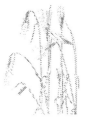

BEER NUMBER

25

Pyramid Espresso Stout
Hart Brewing Company
Kalama and Seattle, Washington

Where else but in espresso-crazy Seattle would you find a *beer* resembling the best a coffeehouse has to offer? This stuff is completely opaque with a thick brown head that you could stand a spoon in. A fruity hop nose gives way to chocolate and coffee overtones which burst out of this brew like lava out of Mount St. Helens. Coincidentally, the exploding Mount happens to be a few miles away from the original Pyramid Brewery where Espresso Stout is brewed.

Brewed without coffee, Hart's brewers create Espresso Stout's café character with rare black malts and special-roast barleys usually associated with Irish stouts. Tempered with caramel and Munich malts, Espresso Stout gives the drinker the rich, mellow flavor of a stout without the acrid tones usually associated with its Irish cousins. Espresso Stout is shipped unpasteurized in 22 oz. (650 ml) bottles and kegs to maximize its fresh, smooth flavor. Jet black, full bodied, and satisfyingly dense, the brewers recommend you enjoy the stout at room temperature on nights as black as the brew itself.

I haven't yet tried this ale with whipped cream and shaved chocolate, but the night is young. And dark.

BEERSTORY   Espresso Stout was originally known as Pyramid Sphinx Stout. In order to take advantage of the craze for espresso coffee, the name was changed in 1994. Crossing labels with Seattle's two favorite beverages proved to be a boon to Hart Brewing Co.

The original Hart Brewery was founded in 1984 by Beth Hartwell, whose name inspired the name of the company. The first barrels rolled out of the brewery in a converted turn-of-the-century general store on First Avenue in Kalama, Washington. Beth and her husband, Tom Baune, had little brewing or business experience. They were located, however, down-stream from Mount St. Helens with her inexhaustible supply of pristine water. Over the mountains lay the Yakima Valley, home to ninety percent of America's hop production. Washington's main wheat and malting facil-ities lay just up the road in Vancouver.

The Hart Brewery was in the center of a pyramid between water, malt, and hops. Before long, the brand name of Hart beers became Pyramid, after those crazy Egyptians and their brewing tradition. When Hart intro-duced Pyramid Wheaten Ale, it was the first wheat beer to be brewed in America since Prohibition.

Beth and Tom took a chance when few people knew what micro-brewed beer was. But their foresight paid off. Hart Brewing has had a dra-matic growth spurt, and they now sell over a hundred thousand barrels a year. They've built a gorgeous new brewery and brewpub in downtown Seattle, southwest of the Kingdome. The pub has stately wood timbers and tables and serves a casual array of pub fare. Giant glass windows offer diners a dramatic view of the brewing process while they enjoy fresh Pyramid and Thomas Kemper beers on tap. Tours are offered seven days a week.

FOOD RECOMMENDATIONS   This beer is a meal in itself. It can also be enjoyed with hearty Italian foods, steaks and rich stews, or poured over vanilla ice cream. For those with a real sweet tooth, serve with chocolate cake. Serve Espresso Stout at room temperature.

RECOMMENDED RELATED BEERS   The Pyramid lineup does not contain one bad beer. They use only classic natural ingredients, and their fruit beers are made from natural extracts of fruit purees. All are unpasteurized. I recommend Pyramid Pale Ale, Pyramid Porter, Wheaten Bock, Kälsch, Snowcap Ale, Hefeweizen, and Apricot Ale. Hart also owns Thomas Kemper Brewery in Poulsbo. I recommend Thomas Kemper WeizenBerry, Hefeweizen, and White.

SPECIFICATIONS   A bargain at $2.79 recommended price per 22 oz. (650 ml) bottle. Alcohol content is 4.5 percent by weight, 5.6 percent by volume. Espresso Stout is brewed at the Hart Brewing Co. in Seattle, 1201 First Avenue South, Seattle, WA 98134. For brewery and tour info dial 206-68-BEERS. E-mail: pyramid@HartBrew.com. Web Sight: http://www.Hart-Brew.com.

BEER NUMBER

26

Pilsner Urquell
Pilsner Urquell-Plzen
Plzen, Czech Republic

Whenever you drink a pilsner beer that's not Pilsner Urquell, you're drinking an imitation. These folks invented the pilsner style. Period. Czech president Vaclav Havel has called Pilsner Urquell "a national treasure." And I'm sure millions of people echo that sentiment hourly when they pop the top of the world's first pilsner beer and golden lager. This beer is great in the bottle and even better if you can find it on tap. Its fragrant, per-fumey hop aroma defines the style with Saaz hops grown in the Zatec region. The beer is a malty potion, well balanced with a complex palate that is rich yet thirst quenching.

Pilsner Urquell is brewed with water from artesian wells deep below the brewery, and it's made with the same strain of yeast that's been used in making pilsner for two centuries.

BEERSTORY   Few other beers have spawned so many imitations. Anytime you drink a mass-produced American barley pop, you're drinking a pale duplication of a Pilsner Urquell. The golden color and the champagnelike sparkle are often copied but rarely reproduced.

In 1292, Franciscan monks began brewing beer in Pilsen in the Bohemia region of what is now the Czech Republic. Over the years, the brewers in Pilsen continued using the same strain of yeast first used by the monks in the thirteenth century. In 1842 the brewers of Pilsen combined their talents to build a single large brewery and to devise a new bottom-fermentation method, which cooled their beers and allowed the yeast to drop to the bottom of the vat during fermentation. The result was the world's first pilsner—a golden lager considerably different from the darker cloudy ales typical of the time. This technique touched off a brewing revolution that forever changed the way most brewers make beer.

In the 1860s new railroad routes helped Pilsner Urquell become a favorite throughout Europe. With the rapid spread of the style, the brewers of Pilsner rechristened their brewery in 1898, combining the name of their town with the German word *urquell* meaning "original source."

Pilsner Urquell was first imported to the United States in 1873. Czech and Slovak immigrants helped the beer's popularity surge, and by 1914 it was the bestselling import in the United States. The beer's international presence declined when the brewery suffered heavy damage during World War II and the Communist government failed to maximize the beer's potential. Today, Pilsner Urquell is enjoying a resurgence of international recognition among beer lovers.

FOOD RECOMMENDATIONS   Pilsner Urquell is a golden thirst quencher that complements almost any food. Try it with barbecue or spicy Mexican food, use it in beer soup, or as a meat marinade.

RECOMMENDED RELATED BEERS   There are a few microbrewed American-made pilsners that are very good. One is Baderbraü Pilsner, made by Pavichevich Brewing Co., a Chicago microbrewery. It embodies the crisp thirst-quenching power of Pilsner Urquell with the gorgeous floral aroma of Saaz hops.

SPECIFICATIONS   I've seen six-packs of Pilsner Urquell sold from $5.99 to $8.99. I've seen the 22 oz. (650 ml) bottles sold from $1.99 to $3.99. The alcoholic content of Pilsner Urquell is 4.4 percent by volume. It is brewed by Plzensky Prazdroj, 30497 Plzen, Czech Republic. Telephone: (019) 227283. It is imported to the United States by Guinness Import Co., Six Landmark Square, Stamford, CT 06901-2704. Telephone: 203-359-7247.

BACKGROUND: THE STORY OF THE *REAL* BUDWEISER

Another famous Czech pilsner is made in the city the Germans call Budweis, or as the Czechs say, "Ceské Budêjovice." Long before "this Bud's for you" entered the American lexicon, the city of Budweis was the home of the Royal Court Brewery of Bohemia. It was also home to forty-three other breweries.

The breweries in Budweis were quick to jump on the pilsner bandwagon in the mid-1800s. One of the breweries in Budweis is named Budejovicky Budvar. Their beer was known far and wide on the Continent as Budweiser Budvar. When German immigrant Adolphus Busch began producing a beer named Budweiser at his Anheuser-Busch brewery in St. Louis, Missouri, a legal battle ensued. That battle is still being fought in courts, one hundred years later.

Long ago, the two breweries reached an agreement giving the Czech brewer the right to use the Budweiser name in Europe and the former Soviet Union. Anheuser-Busch, who, er, uh, *borrowed* the name from the original, agreed to sell its Budweiser in the United States and Latin America. That agreement worked fine in the days when it took a cargo steamer full of beer bottles three weeks to travel from the United States to Europe.

But in today's overnight, international markets, poor little old Anheuser-Busch is cursing the day that they signed that agreement. So when the Czechs embraced democracy and decided to sell off thousands of their government-owned industries, there weren't enough beers at the factory to quench the thirst in the Anheuser-Busch boardroom for the Budvar brewery. The Americans wanted to buy the Czech beer maker and their trademark rights to Budweiser. Finally, "This Bud's for You" would be heard from Portugal to Poland.

There's only one not-so-simple problem. The proud Czechs in the southern town of Ceské Budejovice think the American brewing giant will suck the charm as well as the profits out of their brewery. And besides, as one man says, "I like Americans, their culture, their films. But I know that American beer doesn't reach the quality of Czech beer. It's much poorer, much weaker."

The only market where the two Buds go head to head is in Great Britain. Surveys conducted there have shown the Czech Budvar to be one of the top-rated beers; American Budweiser is dead last.

Anheuser-Busch is trying to win over the Czechs. They built a million-dollar cultural center, sponsored a sports team, opened a marble-floored restaurant, and they're even handing out scholarships and English lessons. Of course, Bud sells over thirteen million cans an *hour*, so a million bucks can't mean too much to them.

Anheuser-Busch founder Adolphus Busch so admired the small Czech brewery that he took their name for his beer in the middle of the nineteenth century. After marrying into the Anheuser family, Busch's Budweiser was born in 1876. Busch thought the prestigious beer name would sell well to the Old World immigrants who populated St. Louis. In another case of *borrowing*, Busch took Budvar's slogan, "The Beer of Kings," and changed it to the now-familiar "King of Beers."

As soon as Busch began to brew Budweiser he was sued by the Czech brewery. The battle over the Budweiser trademark employed stables of lawyers and raged in dozens of countries for decades. A settlement was reached, and each company pledged to stay out of the other's territory. But as new markets opened, whoever got there first registered the Budweiser name; whoever got there last sued.

Under the eighty-four-year-old agreement, American Budweiser is shut out of the beer-guzzling nations of Germany and Austria. It is sold under the name Bud in France, Italy, Spain, and other western European countries. After winning a court battle, Budweiser is allowed to be sold in Great Britain.

As it stands today, the Czech government is drawing up privatization papers for the brewery. Other European brewers are also scratching at the door, simply as a way to keep big, bad Bud off their continent. Until then, the Europeans can still raise a glass and say, "This Budvar's for us!"

BEER NUMBER

27

Oasis Capstone ESB (Extra Special Bitter)
Oasis Brewery
Boulder, Colorado

Silver Medal: Great American Beer Festival, 1994
Gold Medal: World Beer Cup, 1996

By now, most malt hounds know that the Egyptians went *tuts* over beer, but the folks at Oasis have stretched that concept out to its delicious extreme. As one who believes that you can never have too many hops in beer, Capstone ESB is a Sphinx come true.

Holy Cleopatra! The rich herbal nose of Capstone emanates lavender and honey and takes you back to the time of Tutankhamen. The first taste is buttery and sweet with a substantially thick mouth feel. It's got that lightning-electric bubbliness that reeks of the ozone-laden Rocky Mountains from whence it came. Once you forget the pharaohness and hieroglyphs on the label, you realize how true to style this Extra Special Bitter is—a sweet, malty start followed by a slow awakening of the bitter buds on your tongue. This beer lasts and lasts.

The brewer says: "Capstone ESB is by far the best recipe I've ever developed—often imitated, this ale has no equal in the market today. It's a powerful interpretation of an English ESB made with generous quantities of the finest domestic ingredients."

BEERSTORY   The eye on the pyramid commands you to buy. Actually, the cap-stone is the pinnacle, or top, of the pyramid. The proverbial Eye of Re!

Approaching the Oasis Brewery in Boulder, you're not sure whether you're walking into some 1920s movie starring Rudolph Valentino or actually stepping back into ancient Egypt. This brewery is one of the premier microbreweries in the country. Not only that, but they sure got a cool concept going. Their labels would make an Egyptologist squeal with delight. The hieroglyphs spell out Re knows what. The gorgeous wood, marble, and brass interior of the restaurant give you the feeling that you're going to be at the bar for a while.

George Hanna opened the Oasis Brewery and Restaurant in 1991 after a long career as a rock-'n'-roll singer. He spent $2.2 million to remodel a huge old tavern and added a fantastic faux-stone relief of a pharaoh in a barge behind the bar. The menu features the usual sandwiches and pizzas along with gourmet treats such as grilled polenta over ratatouille and salmon with buerre blanc.

Most importantly, Hanna added a brewery. He put it on the fancy dance floor of the former club and left up the disco lights. Apparently those flashing lights can be quite inspirational when brewing up beers to honor the ancient Egyptians.

FOOD RECOMMENDATIONS   ESB has a way of cutting through any food and refreshing any thirst. Great for barbecue, spicy foods, strong cheeses, and picnic lunches.

RECOMMENDED RELATED BEERS   Like many great breweries, these folks don't make a bad beer. I recommend Oasis Pale Ale, Tut's Brown Ale, Oasis Zoser Oatmeal Stout, and Scarab Red Ale.

SPECIFICATIONS   I purchase Oasis Capstone ESB for $3.99 for a 22 oz. (650 ml) bottle, $7.99 for a six-pack of 12 oz. bottles. I've seen it on sale for less. Alcoholic content is about 5 percent by volume. Capstone ESB is brewed by Oasis Brewery & Restaurant, 1095 Canyon Road, Boulder, CO 80302. Telephone: 303-449-0363.

BACKGROUND: A BITTER PRIMER

Bitter is a highly hopped pale ale that grabs the tongue. It is usually light in body and low in alcohol. Bitter is traditionally straw colored, but some may be on the ruddy side of brown. Bitter is fruity with a floral hop character; it's dry with a long hop bitterness in the finish. This is a beer for those who love the noble hop. Bitters may be from 3.8 to 5 percent alcohol by volume. The bitter listed in this book is Oasis ESB.

Only in the topsy-turvy world of beer is the word *bitter* something that sets many a mouth to water. The world is addicted to sugar, and most people would not willingly partake of something called bitter unless forced. Ah, but this is hop bitter, and that's a different kettle of fish.

We have only our tongues to blame. There are four distinct flavors we can sense—sweet, salty, sour, and bitter. But those four simple areas of taste combine to allow us to distinguish thousands of flavors with subtle differences. Beer is particularly enamored of the sweet, sour, and bitter parts of the tongue. The bitter buds are at the back of the tongue, presumably nature's last holdout against us swallowing spoiled mastodon or some such.

Bitter emerged as a style and a tradition in British pubs in the early 1900s. It obviously was not designed by a marketing agent but sort of took on a life of its own over the years. Bottled beer, which was thought to be more sophisticated, was called pale ale. The same beer, when dispensed from kegs and served to working blokes in pubs, was called bitter. The other option in the pub was generally a mild, which was less expensive, lighter, and sweeter.

Bitters grew up around the characteristics of noble Goldings hop and the deliciously named Fuggles hops. In the regions where these hops were grown, less restraint was used when throwing hops into the boiling kettle.

A bitter may be designated Best Bitter, Special Bitter, or Extra Special Bitter depending on the dramatic tendencies of the brewery. In Great Britain there are over two hundred different bitters to sample from.

A great bitter can be a religious experience. As North American microbrewers are so prone to delicious excess, bitter has become a popular style here as well. Every microbrewery worthy of its brewing license will have a bitter on hand.

As the hop heads say: "Bitter comes out better beer."

BEER NUMBER

28

Schlenkerla Rauchbier
Brauerei Heller-Trum, Schlenkerla
Bamberg, Germany

Silver Medal: World Beer Championship, 1995

Rauchbier means "smoked beer" in German, and if you love smoked foods, this is your beer. On the other hand if you don't like smoked food, you will probably hate this beer. As Mr. Trum, the fifth-generation owner of the Schlenkerla Brewery, states, "We don't make beer for everyone, you like it—or you don't."

To get the unique flavor of Schlenkerla Rauchbier, the malt is smoked over an open wood fire. The process starts in a barn in the brewery yard that is stacked high with neat ricks of split beechwood taken from a nearby forest. The beechwood fire is below ground level in a cast-iron hatch in the wall. Above is the small whitewashed building that is the smokehouse. Inside, the grains sit on a mesh screen and the smoke rises through, swirling like a mist and smelling like an autumn bonfire. The malt is made twice a week. The beer is made entirely from smoked malt, unpasteurized, bottom fermented, and matured for seven weeks.

The taste is SMOKY! The beer has a light head, cloudy dunkel color, very slight smoke nose, and DEEP smoke flavor. It tastes of slow-smoked ham cooked in ancient fireplaces. When I close my eyes I see carbon-tinged castle walls and salty smoked boar gracing a twenty-foot-long king's table. The beer has a dryness and a smoky palate that lingers long in the finish.

BEERSTORY   The label on this beer is almost indecipherable. Written in red and black letters in some ancient font, it says "Aecht Schlenkerla Rauchbier (ges. gesch.) Märzen." *Aecht* is Old German for "real." Schlenkerla is the name of the beer, and *rauch* means the beer is smoked. Marzen is beer style. So it says in English: "Real Schlenkerla smoked beer, Marzen style.

The Heller-Trum brewery was founded in 1678. The world-classic rauchbier has its origins in the Schlenkerla Tavern in Bamberg, when it was a brewpub. The Hellers were the early tenants. The Trums are the present owners and have been there for five generations. In the early days, the beer was taken to nearby caves in the hill called Stephansberg for lagering. Eventually, the need for space led to the brewhouse being moved to Stephansberg as well.

FOOD RECOMMENDATIONS   If you want a double-smoked treat, eat with smoked salmon, barbecued or smoked meat, smoked cheeses, and the like. I've marinated chicken and shish kebabs in this beer overnight to won-drous, piquant effect, though it saddened me to use such a great beer as a marinade as opposed to pouring it down my throat. Fortunately, I had several bottles left to wash down the meal the next day.

RECOMMENDED RELATED BEERS   The peat-smoked Adelscott Bièr au Malt à Whisky from the Fischer Brewing Co. in France compares favorably with Schlenkerla because of its musky peat-smoked flavor. Rogue Ales in Oregon also makes a great rauchbier called Rogue Smoke.

SPECIFICATIONS   I paid $3.49 for a 16.9 oz. (500 ml) bottle. Alcoholic content is 4 percent by weight, 5 percent by volume. Schlenkerla Rauch-bier is made at Brauerei Heller-Trum, Schlenkerla, 6 Dominikaner Strasse, 8600 Bamberg, Germany. Telephone: (0951) 56060. It is imported by B. United International, 75 North Central Avenue, Elmsford, NY 10523. Telephone: 914-345-8900. E-mail: 735-5053@mcimail.com.

BACKGROUND: A SMOKED BEER PRIMER

Smoked beer is called *rauchbier* in German, and the technique dates back to 1678. Rauchbier is made with malt that has been smoked over beechwood, oak, or alder. Some smoked beers utilize malt that has been smoked over dried peat. Peat-smoked beers are deeply smoky. One rauchbier brewery plunges white-hot rocks into their brewkettle.

A smoked beer may have just a hint of woodsmoke flavor or else taste like mouthwateringly fresh smoked meat or cheese, to which the beer makes a perfect accompaniment. Rauchbier also makes a great marinade for barbeque. Alcohol contents vary.

Wood-Smoked Beer   Once upon a time, all beers were smoked beers, because malt was dried and wort was boiled over open flames. Scotch whisky is still made with malt dried over burning peat.

Smoked beer, or rauchbier, may be a little hard to find, but it's worth the search. The beers capture a smoky richness that is so desirable in food. Rauchbier has a *basso profundo* note that is as unusual as beer comes. It tastes of deeply smoked, finely prepared beef or salmon. The most famous of rauchbiers come from Bamberg, Bavaria, where the Schlenkerla brewery smokes its malt using the beechwood from the local forests. Here, there are nine breweries in a town of seventy thousand, and the local brewpub was founded in 1536. All make different styles of rauchbier, from a golden lager to a *marzenbier* (March beer).

While most smoked beers come from Germany, there is wood-smoked beer produced in Grodzisk, Poland. Local people claim the beer has been produced in the same brewery since 1300. This beer—called Grodzisk— is made from fifty percent smoked, malted wheat.

Of course, if there's a unique beer style anywhere in the world—no matter how obscure—you can be sure some North American microbreweries will pick it up. From Alaska to Oregon to Vermont, a few adventurous craft breweries are bringing the roasty, rich rauchbier to American consumers, fresh and moderately priced.

Stone Beer   Some smoked beer is made by gingerly smoking grain over an open fire. Others are made when white-hot rocks are plunged into the kettle. The tradition dates back to a time when it was impossible to construct large kettles out of metal. The only way to get a large amount of liquid hot was to shovel nearly molten rocks into a wooden kettle. Agrarian home brewers in Northern Europe used this method of "boiling stones" until the mid-1800s.

In the 1980s, a small brewery in Coburg, Bavaria, was looking for a unique beer that would boost its sales. The owner, Gerd Borges, heard of a beer made with heated stones. Borges found a quarry in southern Austria that had mined rocks for this exact purpose until World War I. The stone from the quarry is called graywacke. It's a type of sandstone that can stand very intense heating and cooling without shattering.

Borge started making stone beer in 1982. To brew it, small boulders are heated over a beechwood fire for twelve hours until they are white-hot. When the stones are 2,200 degrees Fahrenheit, a crane lifts them into a hatch in the brewhouse, where they are lowered into the kettle. The wort, which is half wheat malt, is close to boiling when the stones are put in and comes to boil immediately afterward. The angrily crackling brew fills the room with steam and instantly caramelizes the malt.

The stones become coated with the caramelized malt. When they cool, they are placed in the lagering tanks so the burnt sugar on the stones primes the brew. The beer, Rauchenfels Steinbier, is a true labor of love that is worth the Herculean effort it takes to produce. After all, everybody must get stoned!

Peated Beer   Peat is partially decayed vegetable matter found in marshes and bogs in various parts of the world, most notably Scotland. It is dried and used for fuel. Peat gives the finest Scotch whiskies their notable flavor.

Scotch whisky is also very popular in France. In the early 1980s, the giant French brewer, Fischer, began production of a peat-smoked beer in their Adelshoffen brewery near Strasbourg. The beer is called Adelscott Bière au Malt à Whisky and has a unique smoked flavor due to the peat.

Several American microbreweries use peat-smoked malts in their beers. Though not as assertive as its Euro counterparts, hints of peat-smoked malt may be tasted in Old Bawdy Barley Wine, brewed by Pike Place Brewery in Seattle. Here the smoked flavor is used as a subtle seasoning.

BEER NUMBER

29

Rogue Old Crustacean
Rogue Ales
Newport, Oregon

Silver Medal: Great American Beer Festival (GABF), 1992
Gold Medal: GABF, 1993
Bronze Medal: World Beer Championship, 1994

Old Crustacean reeks of a fine, tawny port. Bold. There's a deep note, almost basso profundo. The palate is amaretto with an alcohol sweetness. It's tart and dry in the finish—the signature of Rogue's proprietary Pacman yeast, which eats the simple sugars and leaves behind the others. This brew is a potion of elaborate flavors. It's almost overwhelming in its presence—each sip demands the drinker's concentration. These tiny eight-ounce bottles contain as much complexity, balance, and ballsy beer flavor as a six-pack of some other beers.

Old Crustacean barley wine is composed of eight malts and two hops. The label is graced by a drawing of a Belgian shrimper "who still pulls his nets from the ocean astride a draft horse." The oxygen-absorbing caps eliminate the crapshoot of off-flavors that may pop up during shipping and storing. This stuff is potent. One or two of these in an evening should be enough for any Rogue.

BEERSTORY   See Rogue Shakespeare Stout for the complete story of Rogue Ales.

FOOD RECOMMENDATIONS   This beer is food. I would drink it with strong cheese, fresh crustaceans, as an aperitif, or with smoked salmon.

RECOMMENDED RELATED BEERS   I recommend every Rogue Ale. See Rogue Shakespeare Stout (beer no. 3) for a complete list of Rogue Ales.

SPECIFICATIONS   I paid $1.99 for a 7 oz. (207 ml) bottle of Old Crustacean. That may sound like a lot, but this stuff is as good as it gets, and it's several times stronger than most beers. The alcoholic content is 11.36 percent by volume. Old Crustacean is brewed by Rogue Ales. Their mailing address is 3135 SE Ferry Slip Road, Newport, OR 97365. Telephone: 541-867-4131. E-mail: rogue@pstat.com. Web page: http//realbeer.com/rogue.

BACKGROUND: A BARLEY WINE PRIMER

Not for the weak of heart, barley wine is a rich, potent beer with an alcohol content that may reach as high as 12 percent by volume. Its flavor may resemble a fine sherry, and its color may be brick red to mahogany—slightly lighter than porter. A malt lover's dream, a lite lover's nightmare. Best enjoyed as an aperitif, with dessert, or as a nightcap, barley wine is about as strong as ale gets.

The strongest beer ever recorded in the *Guinness Book of Records* up until the 1990s was a barley wine made by the Cornish Brewing Co. in December 1986. It was called Doomsday II and packed a beery wallop of 15.86 percent alcohol by volume. The barley wines listed in this book are Old Crustacean and Bigfoot Barleywine Style Ale.

Wine is made from grapes, beer from barley. Thus the term *barley wine* is an oxymoron along the lines of jumbo shrimp. To further complicate matters, bureaucrats at Alcohol, Tobacco, and Firearms never heard of the stuff until the microbreweries started making it in the early 1980s. And no good bureaucrat would let a product made from barley be labeled wine. So the English may sell us a barley wine, but the Americans may only sell us a "barley wine-style ale."

Whatever it's called, barley wine is the sublime zenith of a malt-lover's dream. The term originated in England, back when everybody made their own beer. Barley wine simply meant the best—and usually the strongest beer—that a brewer concocted.

Bass No. 1 Barley Wine was the first commercial beer to use the term back in 1903. Bass still makes old No. 1, but today they're getting a run for their barley from upstart American microbrewers. One brewer, Dock Street, in Philadelphia, takes the style to its logical conclusion, brewing with wine yeast. (I've known home brewers to make the stuff with champagne yeast. Is nothing sacred?)

Barley wine is usually an ale that tops out between 6 and 12 percent alcohol. It is usually, but not always, sold in seven-ounce bottles. Barley wine is usually a brewer's pièce de résistance. It is, after all, the ultimate extreme in barley brewing. Inspiring ale yeast to make great quantities of alcohol takes patience, skill, and a deep understanding of the brewer's art.

In the old days, before the term *barley wine* came into being, breweries simply designated their strongest beer by branding XXXXX on the barrel. Brewers matured the ale in casks for up to eighteen months. The casks were periodically rolled around the yard to wake up the sleeping yeasts, getting more boost in the alcohol content.

Once again expressive Anglo vernacular comes into play when discussing barley wine. My favorite moniker is the Yorkshire term *stingo*.

The barley wine revival in the United States began in 1975 when Anchor Brewing Co. in San Francisco began making their seasonal Old Foghorn. Soon many others were following in Anchor's footsteps. I just had some Old Foghorn on draft the other night, and I recommend it highly.

Not for breakfast, and certainly not for the weak of heart, barley wine is the apex of the brewer's art.

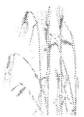

BEER NUMBER
30

Rodenbach Belgian Red Ale
Brouwerij Rodenbach
Roeselare, West Flanders, Belgium

Rodenbach is an exquisite red ale—sometimes called the "Burgundy of Belgium." You would swear that there were cherries in this beer, not only from the red color but from the tart and vinous nose and dry, fruity flavor that is also found in krieks. But this is a result of the fermentation process and the yeast, which is a combination of five different strains.

The reddish-brown Rodenbach is stored in huge oak barrels for eighteen months, where it mingles with *acetobacters*, a type of yeast that has lived in the wood of this brewery for 150 years. The brewery contains about a dozen rooms with three hundred of these gigantic tuns, each one holding from 4,000 to 16,000 gallons of beer. The barrels give the beer its color and distinctive sourness. The brewery employs four coopers who maintain the tuns with numbered staves, hoops, reeds, and beeswax for sealing.

Rodenbach is brewed from four malts; a pale malt from summer-grown barley; two and six-row malts from winter barley; and a reddish crystal malt.

This beer tastes as good as it smells. It's transcendentally sour and acidic but refreshing and palatable. The sourness does not linger. It is complex and tangy but soft and rich. Hints of wine and sweet fruit lurk among the strong oak overtones.

No one makes a beer like Rodenbach anywhere in the world, and I strongly recommend that you find some.

BEERSTORY   The Rodenbach family comes from West Germany, near Koblenz. In the 1700s Ferdinand Rodenbach came to Roeselare as an army surgeon. The family occupies an eminent, even exalted, place in the history of medicine, statesmanship, literature, and brewing in Belgium. Alexander Rodenbach founded the brewery in 1820.

FOOD RECOMMENDATIONS   Rodenbach is celebrated with Belgian cuisine. The beer is so esteemed by cooks that the brewery publishes a compendium of best recipes inspired by Rodenbach. Some of them include: vegetable soup in veal stock with Rodenbach; onion soup with Rodenbach; ham and mushroom crepes with Rodenbach in the batter; mussels in broth with Rodenbach and cream; monkfish with thyme, bay leaves, and tomato steeped in Rodenbach; beef stew with a base of Rodenbach; Cornish hens with hop shoots, vegetables, and Rodenbach sauce; and pork chops with Rodenbach and prunes.

RECOMMENDED RELATED BEERS   Rodenbach makes a Grand Cru, a spicy brew that is aged two years, and Alexander Rodenbach, sweetened with cherry syrup.

SPECIFICATIONS   Rodenbach is one of the more expensive beers, but you get what you pay for. The expense of aging a beer for eighteen months and maintaining antique wooden tuns is enormous. I pay about $4.29 for a 12 oz. (355 ml) bottle of Rodenbach and never regret it. The alcoholic content of Rodenbach is 4.6 percent by volume. Rodenbach is brewed by Brouwerij Rodenbach, 133-141 Spanje Straat, 8800 Roeselare, Belgium. Telephone: (051) 22 34 00. It is imported by Vanberg & Dewulf, 52 Pioneer Street, Cooperstown, NY 13326. Telephone: 607-547-8184.

6

Beers
Thirty-one Through Forty

BEER NUMBER

31

McAuslans Griffon Brown Ale
Brasserie McAuslan
Montreal, Quebec, Canada

Silver Medal: BTI World Championship, 1994

One of the best of this style that I've come across, McAuslans Griffon is more than a brown ale. It's mahogany brown and medium bodied, thirst quenching and light in a pleasant sort of way—hoppy, sweet, and clean, malty up front, with a long, warming finish.

Brewed in the tradition of English brown ales, but fresher, hoppier, and stronger. The nutty flavors come from the British Carastan and roasted barleys. A fine brown.

Owner and brewmaster Peter McAuslan says: "Griffon Brown is not our first beer, nor is it our bestselling. But it's a favorite of the brewery. It's the beer we would make if we were making beer just for ourselves."

BEERSTORY   McAuslan Brewing rolled out their first ales in 1989. They quickly established themselves as Quebec's foremost microbrewery. Since that time, the brewery has introduced five beers.

Peter McAuslan was a home brewer for twenty-five years. He quit his job as senior administrator at Dawson College and dedicated himself to turning his dream of owning a brewery into reality. McAuslans has grown from four employees to forty, but the company still has a commitment to being active in the community, supporting the arts, local events, and charities.

FOOD RECOMMENDATIONS   Brown ales go great with any cuisine. Try Griffon Brown with sharp cheddar or Cotswald cheese, wild fowl, pepper steak, or spicy Oriental food. Serve at 55 degrees Fahrenheit in traditional ale glasses.

RECOMMENDED RELATED BEERS   McAuslans also brews two other great beers, St. Ambroise Pale Ale and St. Ambroise Oatmeal Stout.

SPECIFICATIONS   I pay about $6.59 for a six-pack of 11.5 oz. (340 ml) bottles of Griffon Brown Ale. The alcoholic content is 5 percent by volume. McAuslans is brewed at La Brasserie McAuslan, 4850 St. Ambroise, No. 100, Montreal, Quebec, Canada QUE H4C 3N8. Telephone: 514-939-3060. Free tours Wednesday evening. Griffon Brown Ale is imported by All Saint's Brands, 201 Main Street SE, No. 212, Minneapolis, MN 55414. Telephone: 800-587-9272.

BACKGROUND: A BROWN ALE PRIMER

Brown ales were originally mild and light, with a pleasing nut-brown color. Today's brown ales may range from sweet and watery to dry and bitter. They seem to be getting stronger over the years as American microbrewers try their hand at this traditional English style. Usually a pleasant drink after work and for early evening. Brown ales may range from 3.8 to 5 percent alcohol by volume. The brown ale listed in this book is McAuslans Griffon Brown Ale.

Brown ale is not just for breakfast any more. Mild brown ales date to a time when people thought drinking water would kill them. And it did kill many—especially near larger cities like London and Newcastle. The trend to favor beer over water continued well into the twentieth century.

Today's microbrewed brown ale is lightly hopped, medium bodied, a cozy light brown color, mild, sweet and refreshing. Men, women, and children *did* drink low-alcohol, mild brown ale for breakfast in days of yore.

Modern-style brown ales were first developed in the industrial city of Newcastle, in northern England, in 1890. The term *brown* was actually Newcastle Breweries, Ltd., boasting that their unclouded, reddish-brown ale was *lighter*—thus more refined—than the average, considerably darker, brown ales of the era. The nutty flavored Newcastle Brown Ale is one of the most popular bottled beers in Great Britain. It is notably stronger and lighter in color than the mild, sweet brown ales of centuries past. Newcastle was developed by a man incongruously named Colonel Porter. It was first sold in 1927 and won first prize at the Brewers Exposition in London in 1928. Porter's Brown has been immensely popular ever since.

The farther south one travels in England, the darker, sweeter, and milder the brown ales become. These ales date back to a time when people drank such treats as Brown Bettys, which consisted of hot brown ale, brown sugar, cinnamon, and cognac topped with baked apples. Now *that's* a winter warmer.

Like many things American, a number of microbreweries make their own, eccentric, version of a brown. They may range in color from tawny red to deep brown. But to be true to style, a great brown must be only slightly darker than an India Pale Ale.

Belgians also make their own version of a brown ale, which is covered under Belgian Beer.

BEER NUMBER

32

Bigfoot Barleywine Style Ale
Sierra Nevada Brewing Company
Chico, California

Gold Medal: Great American Beer Festival, 1987, 1988, 1992

It ain't easy making barley wine. The intensity of the malts tends to high-light off-flavors. It's concentrated stuff. But Bigfoot makes a big impression. There isn't an off-flavor to be found in this mountain monster. It pours deep copper with a one-finger head. I swear that I can smell the dense Pacific rain forest and cold Sierra pines in this stuff. Its got a thick mouth feel and a raisin-fudge-chocolate taste on the back of the throat. A sweet Belgian lace coats the glass. The ale is dry and chewy, bubble-tingly, carbonic and tart. Bigfoot is well balanced, dense, fruity, extremely rich, intense, with a bittersweet palate.

BEERSTORY   Bigfoot—the monster, not the beer—lives in the Trinity Moun-tains northwest of Chico, home of Sierra Nevada Brewing Company. The brewery's been at the forefront of the microbrewing industry since its incep-tion in 1981. The principle owners of the company, Ken Grossman and Paul Camusi, learned to brew at home before they designed and constructed the first brewery, entirely by themselves, while working full-time jobs.

The original brewery was constructed of converted dairy equipment, often bought at scrap yards. For the first year, all engineering, production, and administrative work was completed by the two partners. Since the first year, the company has experienced steady sales growth and continual plant expansion. Sierra Nevada is currently the largest of the West Coast micro-brewers and is growing at a rate of over fifty percent annually.

To meet demand, a new brewery was constructed in 1989. The lovely brewery also has a taproom where customers can enjoy fine meals along with Sierra's award-winning ales and lagers. The company is located 100 miles north of Sacramento and 165 miles northeast of San Francisco. Worth the trip for some fresh beers straight from the Sierras.

FOOD RECOMMENDATIONS   Bigfoot Barleywine kicks pretty hard to be much of a thirst quencher. I recommend the ale with Gouda cheese, wal-nuts, pecan pie, and oysters.

RECOMMENDED RELATED BEERS   Award-winning Sierra Nevada beers are superlative examples of fresh, natural, Northern California microbrewed beers. I recommend all of their products, including Pale Bock, Celebra-tion Ale, Porter, and Stout.

SPECIFICATIONS   These beers are a great deal at $9.99 a six-pack. The alcoholic content of Bigfoot is 10.1 percent by volume. It's brewed by Sierra Nevada Brewing Co., 1075 East Twentieth Street, Chico, CA 95928. Telephone: 916-893-3520. Restaurant: 916-345-2739.

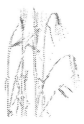

BEER NUMBER
33

Scrimshaw Pilsner Style Beer
North Coast Brewing
Fort Bragg, California

North Coast Brewing is in Fort Bragg, California, about 150 miles north of San Francisco, in Mendocino County. You wouldn't expect a dynamite pilsner from a town hanging into the Pacific Ocean, but this lager is fruity and bold, hoppy as hell, tangy and perfumey, as a good pilsner should be. The hops are up front and floral, and the beer is golden with a creamy head. This is what pilsner tastes like fresh out of the tanks—it's traveled very well to grace my table. Mmmmm good! A great American pilsner and an improvement on the style. As sweet and fragrant as the redwood forests that surround Fort Bragg.

BEERSTORY   Fort Bragg was a whaling port in the 1800s. Today it's a tourist town, about the first large resortlike city on the Pacific north of the Bay Area. The North Coast Brewing Co. set up shop in 1987 in a former mortuary. Their beer, however, is anything but dead. Gazing out at the churning ocean and enjoying their tasty sampler is one memorable experience. The mind immediately begins racing, trying to figure out ways to stay there forever.

FOOD RECOMMENDATIONS   Great pilsners make beautiful marriages with almost any food. But this pilsner is so fragrant and sweetly delicious I recommend it with lighter-flavored foods such as fruits, mild cheeses, fettucini, Greek salads, and river trout.

RECOMMENDED RELATED BEERS   North Coast makes an excellent range of beers. Bottled offerings include Old No. 38 Stout and Red Seal Ale.

SPECIFICATIONS   I paid $1.19 for a 12 oz. (355 ml) bottle of Scrimshaw Pilsner, about $7.99 a six-pack. The alcoholic content is about 4.2 percent by volume. Scrimshaw Pilsner is brewed by North Coast Brewing, 444 North Main Street, Fort Bragg, CA 95437. Telephone: 707-964-2739.

BEER NUMBER

34

Geary's London Style Porter
D. L. Geary Brewing Company
Portland, Maine

A beer so rich you would think there really was a chocolate bar in every bottle. This beer is sublime, a deep mahogany color, with a light body and a subtle blend of toasted-malt flavors. It begs to be drunk slowly, with each drop swished around in the mouth.

Brewed and bottled in Portland, Maine, Geary's London Style Porter was developed from an eighteenth century recipe discovered in London. It was first brewed with the help of Peter Austin and Alan Pugsley, two well-known English microbrewery pioneers. The label features a large Maine lobster that looks like it's just begging to be eaten, washed down with great quaffs of Geary's London Style Porter.

BEERSTORY   The D. L. Geary Brewing Co. was incorporated in October, 1983, by David and Karen Geary, who desired to make great beer on a small scale for local and regional consumption. At the time there were only thirteen microbreweries in the entire United States, almost all of them in California and the Pacific Northwest.

David Geary began a period of training and research in Scotland and England in 1984. With the help of Scottish nobleman and brewer Peter Maxwell Stuart, who arranged introductions, Geary worked in a half-dozen small commercial breweries in the Scottish Highlands and the south coast of England. Geary used this knowledge to design his brewery and formulate his beers.

In the summer of 1984 the Gearys began the long process of finding real estate, designing packaging, raising capital, and acquiring brewing equipment. On December 10, 1986, the first pints of Geary's Pale Ale were sold. New England's first microbrewery had arrived.

FOOD RECOMMENDATIONS   Porters are traditionally gastronomically married to oysters, and Geary's is no exception. Geary's London Style Porter goes great with any Atlantic shellfish or seafood. Also wonderful with Vermont cheddar, Stilton, and Cotswold cheeses. Pour porter over ice cream.

RECOMMENDED RELATED BEERS   Geary's makes a grand Pale Ale and a beer called Hampshire Special Ale. I recommend both beers.

SPECIFICATIONS   I pay about $7.59 for a six-pack of 12 oz. (355 ml) bottles of Geary's London Style Porter. The alcoholic content of London Style Porter is 4.2 percent by volume. London Style Porter is brewed by D. L. Geary Brewing Co., 38 Evergreen Drive, Portland, ME 04103. Telephone: 207-878-2337.

BEER NUMBER

35

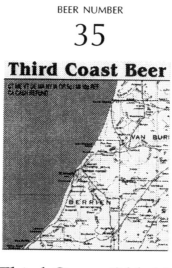

Third Coast Old Ale
Kalamazoo Brewing Company
Kalamazoo, Michigan

Old ale is a traditional English style that most American microbreweries leave alone. It's tough to get a powerful, semisweet ale without getting a cloying sweetness that most people dislike. Plus most American brewers don't have time, space, or money to age an old ale properly.

None of this ever bothered Larry Bell, owner of Kalamazoo's Eccentric Cafe and Brewing Co. *Eccentric* is a nice word used to describe Larry, who loves making excellent beer as much as he enjoys having a great time. Turn the six-pack box of his beer over and you'll read: "So you're the type of person who reads six-pack boxes!" Then Bell goes on to explain his modus operandi, which is "art on the inside, art on the outside."

Folks in Michigan like to think of themselves as living on the Third Coast—the Great Lakes—hence the name Third Coast Old Ale. It's really a barley wine with a toffee nose and a chocolate malt start. It's vaguely reminiscent of cherry wood wainscoting—lush, rich, and Victorian. It's got a gorgeous hop bouquet that is not necessarily found in traditional English old ales. This ale is tawny, rich, and reddish-brown. The brandy of ales. Like all of Kalamazoo's ales, Third Coast is unfiltered, unpasteurized, and naturally carbonated.

BEERSTORY   Larry Bell founded Kalamazoo Brewing Company out of his home-brew supply shop with a fifteen-gallon soup kettle in 1985. Today his brewery is known as one of the premier craft breweries in the country. Kalamazoo has recently added a thirty-barrel brew kettle (930 gallons), and a fifteen-barrel brew kettle to the beloved original two-barrel kettle and the sacred fifteen-gallon soup pot. KBC hopes to be cranking out 24,000 barrels of their excellent beer a year in the near future.

The Eccentric Cafe opened its doors in 1993, becoming the first brewpub in the state of Michigan. The cafe serves light snacks as well as specialty beers that are available nowhere else. You can also pick up home-brewing supplies and T-shirts.

FOOD RECOMMENDATIONS   This beer's too tasty for enjoying with a meal. I recommend Third Coast Old Ale as a digestif, with butterscotch pudding, with caramel popcorn, and sticky buns. A great after-dinner ale. Serve at slightly below room temperature.

RECOMMENDED RELATED BEERS   Bell's beers are even more fun that saying Kalamazoo-zoo-zoo. I strongly recommend Bell's Amber Ale, Bell's Porter, Bell's Pale Ale, and Kalamazoo Stout. Bell's Solsun Ale is available in the summer months, and Bell's Best Brown is available in winter. Expedition Stout, Double Cream Stout, Two Hearted Ale, and Bell's Cherry Stout are brewed in limited quantities during the year.

SPECIFICATIONS   Bell's excellent ales cost a little more, but they are some of the best you can get. I pay about $10.99 for a six-pack of Third Coast Old Ale. The alcoholic content is 10.2 percent by volume. Third Coast Old Ale is brewed by Kalamazoo Brewing Co., 315 East Kalamazoo Avenue, Kalamazoo, MI 49007. Telephone: 616-382-2338.

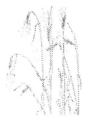

BEER NUMBER
36

Lindemans Gueuze Lambic Cuvée René
Brouwerij Lindemans
Vlezenbeek, Belgium

Long before Dom Perignon introduced the world to champagne, lambic brewers in Belgium were bottling the sparkling gueuze, which is considered to be the height of spontaneously fermented beer.

I open the bronze foil-wrapped green bottle Lindemans Gueuze Lambic Cuvée René by removing the great big cap covering the cork. The beer is as golden as the summer sun and as floral as the deep summer gardens of Europe. It's lemony and sour but light on the tongue, not puckering. This beer will cleanse your palate. It's sweet, apple-tart, bone dry, bubbly, and sensuous—sour to beat the band and tastes like an extremely perfumey hard cider. This may not please everybody. It's a connoisseur's beer—a real combination of champagne, wine, and beer rolled into one refreshing drink. The method in which this beer is brewed makes it sort of a museum in a bottle.

I've found that it really makes a difference to drink this beer in its proper glass. The tulip- and balloon-shaped glasses I used in this tasting really helped release a definite rose and flower character that I couldn't sense when using a regular ale glass containing the same beer from the same bottle.

Cuvée René is a blend of wild yeast lambics—aged from one and a half to two years—to which a percentage of young (six months to one year old) lambic is added. The unfermented sugars in the youngest beer induce a refermentation in the bottle, as is the case with méthode champenoise sparkling wines.

Malted barley and unmalted wheat are the backbone of this complex beer. Their round earthiness is balanced by a shocking wild-yeast seasoning, which replaces the traditional hop bitterness of more conventional beers. Hops aged for three years contribute primarily complexity and their preservative properties. As the gueuze is cellared, the individual sensory characteristics marry and become increasingly complex and balanced.

Like a great Burgundy, traditional gueuze is conditioned in oak before bottling and conditioned for an additional six months to one year before release. Further aging in the final user's cellar for an additional five to ten years or more improves the sophisticated taste.

BEERSTORY   Belgian king Jan Primus, also known as Gambrinus, King of Beer, loved gueuze. Flemish master Peter Brueghel painted local villagers drinking it. Gueuze is also known as the "Burgundy of Brussels," since its elegant, complex, dry flavor is so complimentary to the famous classic cuisine of that city.

In the 180-year history of the brewery, René Lindemans is the sixth generation of his family to pass on the tradition, teaching his heir, son Gert, the art of lambic brewing. Like the great houses of Champagne, which are also a blend of the best casks, Lindemans's reputation rests on the character of his *blends* (cuvées). Beginning in 1994, this beer has been available in limited quantities through Merchant du Vin.

FOOD RECOMMENDATIONS   Great with strong cheese, smoked meat and salmon, and mussels.

RECOMMENDED RELATED BEERS   If you like dry and sour lambics, you might want to try Boons lambics, which are about the sourest beers around. I also recommend other offerings by Lindemans such as Kriek Lambic, Pêche, and Framboise.

SPECIFICATIONS   This is one pricey beer, selling for about $15 for a 25.4 oz. (750 ml) champagne-size bottle. A treat for any occasion. The alcoholic content of Cuvée René is about 5 percent by volume. Lindemans

Cuvée René is brewed by Brouwerij Lindemans, 257 Lenniksebaan, 1712 Vlezenbeek, Belgium. Telephone: (02) 596 03 90. It is imported by Merchant du Vin, 140 Lakeside Avenue, Seattle, WA 98122-6538. Telephone: 206-322-5022. E-mail: info@mdv-beer.com.

BEER NUMBER

37

Oasis Zoser Oatmeal Stout
Oasis Brewery
Boulder, Colorado

Silver Medal: Great American Beer Festival, 1992
Silver and Bronze Medal: GABF, 1993
Gold Medal: World Beer Cup, 1996

The folks at Oasis Brewery use premium ingredients and long maturation times to bring out the best in their beers. Owner and masterbrewer George Hanna says: "Brewing great beer is like culinary or other art forms, where care, patience, and ingredients used with a flair produce the best." I'd have to agree.

Zoser Stout has little head but a grapey-fruity aroma to die for. It's as syrupy as one would expect from a dense oatmeal stout, but extremely complex with caramel aftertones. These folks tap into some ancient Egyptian magic that is irresistible. The beer finishes with one wishing it never had to end. Like finishing a really good book, there's a certain melancholy. Fortunately, there's always another. And another . . .

BEERSTORY   Oasis hit upon the Egyptian theme because the history of beer has most of its roots there. Zoser is the first pharaoh to commission a pyramid. For more on the Oasis Brewery see beer no. 27, Oasis Capstone ESB.

FOOD RECOMMENDATIONS   A deep dense stout like this is a meal by itself. I would also recommend this beer with Italian foods, traditional English fare, beef, Irish Blarney cheese, and strong-flavored seafood.

RECOMMENDED RELATED BEERS   All Oasis beers are like sustenance at an oasis. I recommend Oasis Capstone ESB, Tut's Brown Ale, Pale Ale, Blueberry Ale.

SPECIFICATIONS   I purchase Oasis Zoser Oatmeal Stout for $3.99 for a 22 oz. (650 ml) bottle, $7.99 for a six-pack of 12 oz. (355 ml) bottles. I've seen it on sale for less.

Alcoholic content is about 5 percent by volume. Zoser Oatmeal Stout is brewed by Oasis Brewery & Restaurant, 1095 Canyon Road, Boulder, CO 80302. Telephone: 303-449-0363.

BEER NUMBER

38

Witkap-Pater Abbey Singel Ale

Brouwerij Slaghmuylder
Flanders, Ninove, Belgium

I wouldn't pretend to pronounce the name of the brewery correctly. Thank goodness I can (mis)pronounce Witkap, which means "white head," Flemish for towhead. This beer has a penetrating palate with a wheaty-clove taste. It's smoky and delicious. Tastes of spring and summer with a delicious rocky head and a vanilla backthroat. The smell of a perfect summer's day. It's *clean* beyond belief. This blond beer sparkles like champagne and has the typical fruity nose of an abbey-style beer, fairly reeking of banana and berry. Light body with a lemony finish.

Witkap is fermented at very high temperatures and held that way for five days. The beer is aged for five weeks and then centrifuged to remove hop and protein gunk. Candy sugar and new yeast is added before bottling.

BEERSTORY   The Slaghmuylder Brewery is the only surviving brewery in a town of twelve thousand where there were once thirteen breweries. The brewery boasts a functioning steam engine and Anheueser-Busch kegs left behind from World War II. They make the only beer brewed by a layman ever permitted to use the Trappist designation on the label.

The 134-year-old brewery is overseen by three cousins who are descendants of the original founder—Emmanuel Slaghmuylder. The cousins brew the beer according to a recipe first developed at the Drie Linden brewery in nearby Brasschaat. The brewer there developed many celebrated beers for the Trappist monasteries. He was so beloved by the brothers, and his contributions so valued, that they bestowed upon him the special gift of the Trappist designation. The Slaghmuylders bought the Drie Linden brewery in 1981. Though 6 percent alcohol, Witkap is the lightest of the Trappist beers and drunk by the monks at the midday meal.

FOOD RECOMMENDATIONS   Witkap Singel is recommended with seafood—particularly mussels, sole, and turbot. It's also recommend as a sauce for fish made with Witkap, fish stock, cream, and tomato puree. Witkap is great for steaming mussels—just pour some in a pot with some thyme and bay leaves.

RECOMMENDED RELATED BEERS   There are many single Trappist ales available that are on par with Witkap Single. They include Chimay and Orval.

SPECIFICATIONS   Witkap is about $2.29 for an 11 oz. (335 ml) bottle. The alcoholic content is 6 percent by volume. Witkap Singel is brewed by Brouwerij Slaghmuylder in Flanders, Ninove, Belgium.

Witkap Singel is imported by Vanberg & Dewulf, 52 Pioneer Street, Cooperstown, NY 13326. Telephone: 607-547-8184.

BEER NUMBER

39

Black Jack Porter
Left Hand Brewing Company
Longmont, Colorado

Gold Medal: Great American Beer Festival, 1995
Bronze Medal: GABF, 1994

Yesss! This is a London-style porter brewed American micro-style with plenty of bold hop bouquet. It's dark ruby in color, and sweet and clean thanks to the Rocky Mountain spring waters used in brewing. Malty and complex with a lingering chocolate and coffee palate, this porter finishes dry, pure, and supple. This is what the guys in the brewery drink when *they're* thirsty. As the brewer says: "Be happy, Jack!"

BEERSTORY   Left Hand Brewing Co. was founded in 1993 by Eric Wallace and Dick Doore. Both were U.S. Air Force Academy graduates (1984 and 1985, respectively) with home-brewing experience. The Left Handers installed a seventeen-barrel brewery in an old meatpacking plant and were cranking out thirty-five hundred barrels of beer a year by 1995.

The name *Left Hand* comes from the town the founders lived in, Niwot, Colorado. Niwot was a southern Arapaho chief who used to pass the winter in the Boulder Valley with his tribe. His name means "left hand" in Arapaho.

The Left Hand guys are new to the brewing world but have garnered considerable notice, winning seven medals in beer fests in two years. When it's made in batches this small, a great attention to detail is inevitable.

Black Jack Porter was originally named after the leather drinking tankards sealed with resin that were common two centuries ago. There on the label is a jack of clubs and an ace of diamonds—a blackjack hand. The jack is holding a blackjack tankard. The cap has a left handprint.

Another quote from the brewers: "Brewed to be enjoyed with friends and to stimulate serendipity." I'm feeling serendipitous already.

FOOD RECOMMENDATIONS   Since porter is traditionally drunk with oysters, should Rocky Mountain porter be drunk with Rocky Mountain oysters? That's a decision everyone must make on their own. Great with nuts (from trees), filthy, stinking cheeses, cold cuts, and rich desserts.

RECOMMENDED RELATED BEERS   Left Hand brews three other excellent ales: Sawtooth Ale, an ESB-style that has won several major medals; Juju Ginger Ale, brewed with real ginger; and Motherload Golden Ale, a Scottish ale.

SPECIFICATIONS   I've seen Black Jack Porter sold for $2.99 to $3.99 for a 22 oz. (650 ml) bottle. Alcoholic content of Black Jack Porter is 6.2 percent by volume. It's brewed by Left Hand Brewing Co., 1265 Boston Avenue, Longmont, CO 80501. Telephone: 303-722-0258. E-mail: lefthand@frontrange.net. Web site: http://frontrange.net/lefthand.

BEER NUMBER

40

Redhook Doubleblack Stout
(Brewed With Starbucks Coffee)
Redhook Brewery
Seattle, Washington

Was there ever any doubt that somebody in the Pacific Northwest would finally just pitch the oh-so-trendy coffee right into the microbrewed beer and get it over with? One company, Pyramid Brewing, makes Espresso Stout, which is coffeelike but using only a pure malt blend. Then along comes Redhook Brewery, who made a deal with Starbucks Coffee, and combines two of the Pacific Northwest's most famous products.

Doubleblack Stout is an imperial stout style that smells like the fresh coffee aisle at your grocers but not like perked coffee. There are almond overtones and it's black as sin. It has a small head with tiny bubbles and a sweet, smooth stout palate with a piquant and bitter finish. There's a taste of honey and a touch of wheat.

They say that Doubleblack Stout is the only beer of its kind in the world, and that's a fact! But I started to get a little jittery from the caffeine in a pleasant sort of way about halfway through the bottle. Don't drink this stuff if you want to be quiet and go to bed early. They say it contains only one-third of the caffeine in a regular five-ounce serving of coffee, but there's some kind of magical synergy going on between the coffee and the beer that I found to be marvelous. This beer is definitely conducive to long talks deep into the night. The speedball of beers.

BEERSTORY   Paul Shipman, founder of Redhook, and Gordon Bowker, founder of Starbucks, have known each other since 1980, and they both shared a passion for fresh, quality beer. Shipman, who was a marketing analyst for the winery Chateau Ste. Michelle, decided to start a microbrewery with Bowker. They raised $350,000 and bought a twenty-five-barrel German-made brew kettle and other necessary equipment. Redhook was built in the Ballard neighborhood, an ethnic Scandinavian part of Seattle. On August 1, 1982, Redhook sold its first pint.

By 1986, demand for Redhook and Ballard Beers was so strong that Redhook had outgrown its original brewery. Shipman went to Europe to purchase equipment for a new brewery and brewpub. The new sight was a redbrick building that originally housed the Seattle Electric Railway in 1908 and served as a trolley repair facility. The new brewpub was called The Trolleyman. It opened in 1988.

Redhook had been growing at a clip of forty percent a year, and in 1993 the company purchased a twenty-two-acre site for a new brewing facility in Woodinville, eighteen miles east of Seattle. The new brewery came on line in 1994. Ten of the acres remain as natural wetlands. Recently, Redhook struck a distribution deal with Anheuser-Busch to distribute Redhook, and plans are under way to build several Redhook breweries in different parts of the country.

FOOD RECOMMENDATIONS   In colonial times, coffee and beer were found side-by-side on the breakfast table. Pour Doubleblack Stout over chocolate ice cream. This beer is also a great aperitif. You can serve it in place of coffee.

RECOMMENDED RELATED BEERS   Redhook makes a great line of beers that are widely available and competitively priced. I recommend Redhook ESB, Wheat Hook, Ballard Bitter, Redhook Rye (!), Blackhook Porter, and the seasonal Winterhook.

SPECIFICATIONS   Redhook Doubleblack Stout is available in 22 oz. (650 ml) bottles and sold from $2.29 to $3.99. The alcoholic content is 5 percent by volume. Doubleblack Stout is brewed by Redhook Ale Brewery, 3400 Phinney Avenue North, Seattle, WA 98103. Telephone: 206-548-8000. Web address: http://www.halcyon.com/rh/rh.htlm.

7

Beers
Forty-one Through Fifty

BEER NUMBER
41

Samuel Smith's Old Brewery Pale Ale
Samuel Smith Old Brewery
Tadcaster, Yorkshire, England

Gold Medal: World Beer Championship, 1994

Back in the days before the Industrial Revolution, most beers were dark and cloudy. When sparkling amber beers were introduced they were called pale ales to distinguish them from the porters. Samuel Smith's Old Brewery Pale Ale is the definition of the style.

Sam's Pale Ale pours copper-golden with a half-inch of eggshell white head. Bigger bubbles separate to the edge of the glass while tiny bubbles sparkle like the Milky Way. You can almost smell the caramely-sticky slate fermenters that this beer is born in. There's a hint of butter and a taste of the mysterious, hidden past of England's foggy antiquity.

BEERSTORY   The tiny village of Tadcaster in Yorkshire, England, has three breweries. The most famous in America is Samuel Smith, founded in 1758 and still family owned. The brewery was built to supply ale to the neighboring White Horse Inn, which is also still in operation. For more on the Samuel Smith Brewery see beer no. 7, Samuel Smith's Taddy Porter.

FOOD RECOMMENDATIONS   Yorkshire beer with Yorkshire pudding? Makes sense to me. Goes with rare roast beef, roast chicken, Dungeness crab salad, bouillabaisse, tandoori, and sushi.

RECOMMENDED RELATED BEERS   Samuel Smith does not make a bad beer, and, in fact, most of their products are listed elsewhere in this book. I highly recommend the Famous Taddy Porter, Oatmeal Stout, Imperial Stout, Nut Brown Ale, and Winter Welcome.

SPECIFICATIONS   I pay about $8.59 to $10.99 for a six-pack of 12 oz. (355 ml) bottles of Old Brewery Pale Ale. The alcoholic content is 4.1 percent by weight, 5.2 percent by volume. Samuel Smith's Old Brewery Pale Ale is brewed at The Old Brewery, Tadcaster, Yorkshire, LS24 9DSB, England. Telephone: (0937) 832 225. It is imported by Merchant du Vin, 140 Lakeside Avenue, Seattle, WA 98122-6538. Telephone: 206-322-5022. E-mail: info@mdv-beer.com.

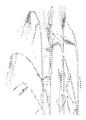

BEER NUMBER

42

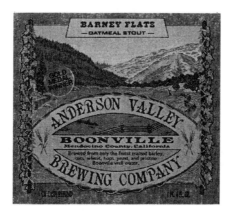

Barney Flats Oatmeal Stout
Anderson Valley Brewing Company
Boonville, Mendocino County, California

Gold Medal for Stout: Great American Beer Festival (GABF), 1990

Barney Flats Oatmeal Stout has a Northern Californian, almost cedar, bouquet. The air around the brewery is teaming with fragrant, floral, and fruity wild scents in this, the heart of California's wine country. Some delicious wild yeasts must slip into Anderson Valley's beers, giving them that oh-so-sweet Northern California essence. Slippery, creamy, dark, and sweet as a Pacific May morning. Soft and complex, this beer could almost be poured over Coco Puffs for breakfast.

Anderson Valley beers are made with pristine waters drawn from an eighty-foot-deep well sheltered directly beneath the brewery. The grains are milled and mashed *overnight*, which gives the beer the fullest flavor possible. These folks brew only about fifty-five hundred barrels of beer a year, and when they do brew, they don't mess around. I recommend a trip to the Buckhorn Saloon, the brewpub located above the brewery in Boonville, two hours and thirty minutes north of San Francisco, in some of the most beautiful country on Earth.

BEERSTORY   The Anderson Valley Brewery is located in Boonville, nestled in a pleasant hilly countryside of apple orchards, vineyards, and redwoods. Boonville was once a remote logging and sheep-ranching station. Hard-working folks there elbowed up to the neighborhood bar for a cold brew after work. After a few beers, the folks decided to invent their own language called Boontling. To keep out-of-towners out of their affairs, the Boontling dialect just kept growing until the folks published their own dictionary. So when you see a sign over the bar that says "It's not just shy sluggin' gorms neemer," it means "It's not just for breakfast anymore," in Boontling.

The Anderson Valley Brewery is built on the site of the original Buck-horn Saloon, which was founded in 1873. Former chiropractor Dr. Kenneth Allen and his wife, Kimberly, resurrected the name for their brewpub, which rolled out its first barrel on December 26, 1987. Although the brewpub and brewery are relatively new, they were designed and built to blend in with the surrounding landscape and look like they've been there for decades.

FOOD RECOMMENDATIONS   This beer is made to complement the brewpub upstairs, which serves specialties such as Deep Enders Chicken made with porter, the Fisherman's Platter made with Wheat, and Chili Con Barney made with the aforementioned stout.

RECOMMENDED RELATED BEERS   Anderson Valley makes many good beers that come highly recommended. Some are named in Boontling. Boont Amber and Belk's ESB both won gold medals in the World Beer Championship in 1995 and bronze medals in Great American Beer Festival the same year. Their other beers are Poleeko Gold Pale Ale, Deependers Dark Porter, and High Rollers Wheat.

SPECIFICATIONS   I paid about $3.29 for a 22 oz. (650 ml) bottle of Barney Flats Oatmeal Stout. It's brewed with pale malt, caramel, and chocolate barleys and blended with wheat and oats. The alcoholic content is 5 percent by volume. Barney Flats Oatmeal Stout is brewed at Anderson Valley Brewing Co., 14081 Hwy. 128, P.O. Box 505, Boonville, CA 95415. Telephone: 800-207-BEER. E-mail: avb@pacific.net. Web site: http//:www.avbc.com/avbc/home.html.

BEER NUMBER

43

Pumpkin Ale
Buffalo Bill's Brewery
Hayward, California

Back in the 1980s most brewers thought that tossing pumpkins into your ale was a sure sign of insanity—even on Halloween. That's because they never met Buffalo Bill Owens. Mr. Owens is responsible for pushing through the legislation that legalized brewpubs in California, setting off a national revolution that is still in high gear. Today, when we can buy beer containing everything from chili peppers to coffee to cranberries, we forget just how revolutionary Pumpkin Ale was. And it should be revolutionary. It was inspired by George Washington, general, scholar, president, and avid home brewer. Washington used pumpkins and other vegetables in brewing.

To taste a Pumpkin Ale is to taste pumpkin pie in a bottle. It's pumpkin-gold in color with a nice whipped-cream head. The allspice jumps right out at you on the first sniff, followed by a piquant hint of real pumpkin. The first sip is definitely pumpkin pie with a bitter bite on the back of the tongue. Next Halloween I'm dressing up as a bottle of Pumpkin Ale.

BEERSTORY   Award-winning photographer Buffalo Bill Owens is the spiritual founder and Godfather of the modern brewpub industry. He agitated the government to legalize the concept and built his own brewery from scratch in 1983. Although Mr. Owens was instrumental in legalizing brewpubs, he missed being the first brewpub owner in California by only a few weeks. (Damn!)

Bill began brewing Pumpkin Ale in 1988. He picked a forty pound pumpkin from his garden, seeded it, baked it at 350 degrees Fahrenheit for three hours and threw it in the mash tun on brew day. The pumpkin pulp produced starches that were converted to sugars and then fermented into alcohol. Allspice is added to the brew to give it a unique flavor.

Bill sold his brewpub to his brewer in 1995 so he could concentrate on publishing his excellent magazines, *BeeR: the magazine*, and *American Brewer*.

FOOD RECOMMENDATIONS   This is a great beer to grace your Thanksgiving table and it's also a great thirst-quencher in the summer. Take along on picnics and barbecues. Enjoy as an aperitif or as a midafternoon restorative. Great with soups, salads, and sandwiches.

RECOMMENDED RELATED BEERS   Buffalo Bill's also puts out an excellent beer called Alimony Ale—"the bitterest beer in America." Bill's CPA was going through a bitter divorce when he thought of the idea of Alimony Ale. To make it the bitterest beer, Bill took an amber beer and tripled the hopping rate from four pounds to twelve pounds per 186-gallon batch. This gave Alimony Ale seventy-two units of bitterness when most American beers have sixteen units. On the original label, Bill ran an advertisement looking for a wife for his CPA. Unfortunately—or maybe fortunately—the CPA still hasn't remarried.

SPECIFICATIONS   I buy Pumpkin Ale and Alimony Ale in 22 oz. (650 ml) bottles that cost between $2.99 and $3.99. The alcoholic content is about 5 percent by volume. Pumpkin Ale is brewed by Dubuque Brewing Co., 500 East Fourth Street Extension, Dubuque, IA 52001. Telephone: 800-787-2739. To find out more about Pumpkin Ale or order *BeeR: the magazine*, or *American Brewer*, call 800-646-2701. Web address: http://and.com/bb/bb.html.

BEER NUMBER
44

Samuel Adams Triple Bock
Boston Beer Company
Boston, Massachusetts

Move over Thomas Hardy's Ale and Samichlaus lager, the *Guinness Book of Records* has a new winner for the world's strongest beer.

You've heard of bock. You've heard of doppelbock. Leave it to brew king Jim Koch to take us over the top with Samuel Adams Triple Bock.

With a bouquet of sherry and alcohol, Triple Bock pours ruby-raisin-brown. The bottle is cobalt blue with 24-karat gold lettering and a sherry cork instead of a cap. No wonder this stuff costs $100 for a case of 8.45 oz. (250 ml) bottles. There's not much of a head to get in the way of the first eager taste. If I didn't know this was beer, I would think I was drinking sherry wine. It's sweet all right, but I can taste the floral perfume of fine hops wafting up the back of my throat. There's a subtle hint of maple syrup, oak, fine spring flowers, and whisky. It's a heavenly flavor I want to last forever, but I wouldn't recommend drinking too many of these in one sitting.

Triple Bock is crafted using ingredients common to many beers—two-row barley malt, Bavarian hops, water, and yeast. But Triple Bock uses four times as much barley as conventional beers, as well as a touch of Vermont maple syrup. The yeasts are a blend of brewer's yeast and champagne yeast. The ale is aged in oak whisky barrels for four months. The brewing process is unique, and Koch has a patent pending on the procedure.

BEERSTORY   Boston Beer Co. introduced Samuel Adams Boston Lager in 1985. Since then, they've basically carved out a niche as the world's biggest microbrewer—an oxymoron if there ever was one. But Adams founder Jim Koch, a third generation brewer, has done more to popularize high-quality all-malt beer than almost anyone. His success is evident by the fact that Samuel Adams beer is available almost everywhere and is a welcome alternative to the offerings in most pubs and taverns.

Koch says about Triple Bock: "The idea was to create a beer that was unique, complex, and so special that it would stretch the definition of beer. We wanted to show people that beer can have all the flavor, character, and nobility of vintage wine and to educate people about the variety and the wonder of beer."

When are we going to get some Quadruple Bock, Jim? We'll probably need a spoon to eat that one.

FOOD RECOMMENDATIONS   This is a beer that should be enjoyed by itself. Any food will simply muck up the flavor. And with such a high alcohol content, Triple Bock is not really meant to be a thirst quencher. I recommend this as an aperitif with a good Cuban cigar.

RECOMMENDED RELATED BEERS   Samuel Adams brews a wide range of beer styles. Try their Cream Stout, Honey Porter, Cherry Wheat, and Cranberry Lambic.

SPECIFICATIONS   You get what you pay for when you pick up an 8.45 oz. (250 ml) bottle of Triple Bock for $4.99. The alcoholic content is 17 percent (!) by volume. Samuel Adams is brewed at a winery in Ceres, California, for the Boston Beer Co., 30 Germania Street, Boston, MA 02130. Telephone: 617-522-3400.

BEER NUMBER

45

Dock Street Bohemian Pilsner
Dock Street Brewing Company
Philadelphia, Pennsylvania

Gold Medal: Annapolis Beer Festival, 1992

Voluptuous Pilsner Beer! It's hard to find a microbrewed American-made pilsner that rivals its Czech counterparts, but here it is. Dock Street Bohemian Pilsner is brewed in the style of the original pilsners of Bohemia in what is now Czechoslovakia. They use enormous amounts of Czech Zatec and German Hallertau hops to give the beer a perfumey, elegant bouquet. The beer is rich golden in color with a soft, complex, and malty palate. It's got a long, dry finish.

BEERSTORY   Dock Street Brewing Company was founded in 1986 by Jeff Ware, who was a restaurateur as well as an artist and sculptor. The original brewmaster at Dock Street was Mortimer Brenner, who was in the business for more than forty years. He has eleven brewing-related patents to his credit and has won many prestigious awards. Mr. Brenner died at the age of 75 in 1987.

FOOD RECOMMENDATIONS   If you're in Philly, I highly recommend that you visit the award-winning Dock Street Brewery & Restaurant. They've got plenty of great dishes that go with their outstanding beer, including roasted and char-grilled meats, fish, game pies, and home baked bread. Dock Street has also recently opened a new restaurant and brewery in Washington, D.C., at Thirteenth and Pennsylvania Avenue.

I've used Dock Street Pilsner as a base for an astounding party-stopping French onion soup. Pour a bottle in with the rest of the recipe.

RECOMMENDED RELATED BEERS   Dock Street bottles two other excellent beers, Dock Street Amber and Dock Street Illuminator Bock. They also brew a wide range of styles available in their brewpubs.

SPECIFICATIONS   I've seen Dock Street Bohemian Pilsner sold for $4.50 to $5.50 a six-pack of 12 oz. (355 ml) bottles and $1.99 to $3.99 for single 22 oz. (650 ml) bottles—a good deal for a fresh Czech-style pilsner. The alcoholic content of Bohemian Pilsner is about 4 percent by volume. Dock Street Bohemian Pilsner is brewed by Dock Street Brewery & Restaurant, 2 Logan Square, Philadelphia, PA 19103. Telephone: 215-496-0413.

BEER NUMBER

46

THOMAS

HARDY'S ALE

VINTAGE 1994

Thomas Hardy's Ale (Vintage 1994)
Eldridge, Pope & Company
Dorchester, Dorset, England

Thomas Hardy's Ale is the beery equivalent of rare cognac. It's bottled with natural yeast to mature in the bottle like fine wine and it will improve with age for an astounding twenty-five years. I've read of old vintages of this beer being sold for thousands of dollars. In the world of beer, that's simply unheard of. Each year's limited bottling is vintage dated, and the first batch of each year's vintage is usually released in July or August.

Thomas Hardy's Ale (Vintage 1994) is so complex that I can *taste* smoked soft cheese, cinnamon, fruit, and coriander by scent alone—without even putting the beer to my lips. The first taste is a shocking melange of sweet barley, musty oak, and raisins, immediately shot through with a puckering bitterness. There's a hint of Madeira and a Rubenesque quality to this small glass of ale. This is English-Gentleman's-Club beer and a fine panatela cigar would set this one up. The label recommends storing the beer for five years before drinking and I imagine that would do a lot to muffle the malty sweetness of the newer brew. I can only dream of drinking a Vintage 1987, 1974, or 1968 . . . Thomas Hardy importer, George Saxon, are you listening?

Thomas Hardy's Ale is brewed with seven pounds of hops per thirty-one-gallon barrel and is made with rare Maris Otter barley malt. Hardy's is fermented for ten days in open square vessels made of wood and lined with copper. After maturation in warm tanks for six weeks, the beer is stored at near-freezing temperatures for five to seven months, then bottled straight from the tank with its natural yeast.

BEERSTORY   In his book *The Trumpet Major*, English poet and novelist Thomas Hardy (1840–1928) waxed poetic about a mythical beer brewed in an imaginary English shire called Wessex. In several other novels, Hardy wrote about a brewery called Casterbridge, which was actually a thinly veiled reference to the Eldridge Pope brewery in Dorchester. Hardy, who lived in Dorchester, was a friend and contemporary of Alfred Pope, first chairman of the brewery. Many say that Pope's strong beers gave Hardy inspiration for his novels.

In 1968 a literary festival was held in Dorchester to commemorate the fortieth anniversary of Hardy's death. Eldridge Pope made a special beer for the occasion that was to be a once-only brew. But Thomas Hardy's Ale became so popular that the brewery began to brew it annually with vintage-dated bottles. It was the strongest brew made in England for many years and won a spot in the *Guinness Book of Records* for a time.

FOOD RECOMMENDATIONS   Hardy's is a robust complement to rich, hearty foods, veined cheeses like Stilton and Huntsman, and rich chocolate desserts. It's an appropriate alternative to an after-dinner liqueur. Sip and savor.

RECOMMENDED RELATED BEERS   Eldridge, Pope & Company brews some excellent beers. I recommend Royal Oak, Pope's 1880 Ale, and Thomas Hardy's Country Ale.

SPECIFICATIONS   As one would expect from a beer meant to be cellared for twenty-five years, Hardy's is not inexpensive. I've seen it sold for over $25 a six-pack of 11.25 oz. (330 ml) bottles, and $4.99 for a single (11.25 oz.) bottle. I recommend cellaring one bottle from every six-pack. To cellar the beer, store at 55 to 60 degrees Fahrenheit in a dark place. Store it upright, as it is not corked.

The alcoholic content of Hardy's is 9.5 percent by weight, 12 percent by volume. Thomas Hardy's Ale is brewed by Eldridge, Pope & Co., Weymouth Avenue, Dorchester, Dorset, DT1 1QT, England. Telephone: (0305) 251251. It's imported by Phoenix Imports, Ltd., 2925 Montclair Drive, Ellicot City, Baltimore, MD 21043. Telephone: 800-700-4ALE.

BEER NUMBER

47

Samichlaus Bier (Vintage 1995)
Brauerei Hürlimann
Zurich, Switzerland

Samichlaus is brewed one day a year, on December 6, which is St. Nicholas Day in Switzerland. It is then lagered for one year and served on the following St. Nicholas Day.

Surprisingly smooth and fresh smelling for a beer that was once listed in *Guinness Book of Records* as the world's strongest beer—14.7 percent alcohol by volume!

Samichlaus has a caramel nose, a minuscule hop bouquet, and is copper-amber in color. The tightly packed dense head and tiny bubbles are very even and precise—as you'd expect from something Swiss. Hops strike you not exactly in a scent but instead in a sort of floral *sensation* as the beer glides to your lips. This beer is aged ten months before bottling for the American market, twelve months for the Swiss. That's what makes this brew rounded and mellow, which belies it's overall effect on the consciousness. It finishes like a good cognac with overtones of port wine, dried fruit, and peppery hop.

If a high-alcohol beer is to be successful, it has to be gentle, sweet, and attractive rather than bold and concussive. The former is far more seductive than the latter. If I didn't know how strong this beer was, I wouldn't have guessed until later—maybe the next morn. There's certainly nothing on the bottle, such as the word *doppelbock*, that would be found on other contenders in this category of potency.

Full bodied, almost creamy, Samichlaus is brewed with two-row summer barley and two varieties of Hallertau hops. A very special yeast has been developed to withstand the stunning effects of the alcohol. The brewing process is a closely guarded secret, but it's no secret that it's an all-natural brew that's long and difficult.

If you want something completely different for Christmas, get Santa to bring you the beer they named after him.

BEERSTORY   Beer has been brewed around Zurich since the so-called Dark Ages. Hürlimann brewery was founded in 1836. It moved to its present location in 1866 to take advantage of the lagering caves in the foothills of the Alps. Hürlimann is known for its exacting research with yeast and has supplied strains to over two hundred breweries worldwide. Their research led them to isolate the yeast in Samichlaus that could tolerate its high alcohol content.

FOOD RECOMMENDATIONS   Samichlaus should be stored and served at cellar temperatures. It's a grand accompaniment to robust foods and to sweets, including chocolate. An excellent alternative to an after-dinner brandy or cordial.

RECOMMENDED RELATED BEERS   If you like these high-alcohol lagers, check out German doppelbocks like Salvator, Optimator, and Celebrator.

SPECIFICATIONS   This beer, besides being one of the highest in alcohol content, is also one of the highest in price. Expect to pay upward of $25 for a six-pack of 12 oz. (355 ml) bottles of Samichlaus. The alcoholic content of Samichlaus is 11.6 percent by weight, 14.7 percent by volume. Samichlaus is brewed at Brauerei Hürlimann, 150 Brandschenke Strasse, 8002 Zurich, Switzerland. Telephone: (01) 288-2626. It's imported by Phoenix Imports, Ltd., 2925 Montclair Drive, Ellicott City, Baltimore, MD 21043. Telephone: 800-700-4ALE.

BEER NUMBER

48

Celebrator Doppelbock
Brauerei Aying
Aying, Bavaria, Germany

Best of Show: California Beer Festival, 1995
Gold Medal: California Beer Festival, 1995
Silver Medal: World Beer Championships, 1994

This beer, graced around the neck with a goat charm on a red-and-white string, is the original party animal. If kick-ass doppelbocks are your thing, you'll love the Celebrator.

Celebrator is inky black with a profoundly dark taste in a rich elixir with a complex fruitiness of roasted malt and whole hop flowers. Drink this beer carefully if you want to remain a celebrator. Three of these and you'll be a stumble-ator.

BEERSTORY   Originally brewed at a monastery in northern Italy, double bock was introduced by Bavarian brewers to compete with bock.

The Ayinger Brewery, makers of Celebrator, was founded in 1878. It was named Small Brewery of the Year at the 1994 World Beer Championships. The brewery is located in Aying, a storybook village of one thousand beer enthusiasts in Munich County, only seventeen kilometers from the center of the capital city.

FOOD RECOMMENDATIONS   Drink with pastries and desserts, roast goose, cured ham, smoked duck, wild turkey, filet with Dijon sauce, chanterelles, tornadoes Rossini, and chateaubriand.

RECOMMENDED RELATED BEERS   Ayinger makes quite a few award-winning beers, including Ayinger Oktober Fest-Märzen, Ayinger Bräu-Weisse, Ayinger Ur-Weisse, Ayinger Maibock, Ayinger Jahrhundert-Bier, and Ayinger Altbairisch Dunkel.

If you enjoy billy-goat-kicking doppelbocks, I recommend Paulaner Salvator, Augustiner Maximator, Spaten Optimator, and, from Austria, the Eggenberger Ur-Bock, which is a high-gravity blond doppelbock.

SPECIFICATIONS   Another pricey brew costing around $12.99 for a six-pack. The alcoholic content of Celebrator is about 6 percent by volume. Celebrator is brewed by Brauerei Aying Franz Inselkammer, 1 Zornedinger Strasse, 8011 Aying, Germany. Telephone: (08095) 8815. It is imported by Merchant du Vin, 140 Lakeside Avenue, Seattle, WA 98122-6538. Telephone: 206-322-5022. E-mail: info@mdv-beer.com.

BEER NUMBER

49

MacAndrew's Scotch Ale
Caledonian Brewing Company
Edinburgh, Scotland

World Champion Scottish Ale: World Beer Championship, 1994

The Scottie dog on the label makes you think of something warm, fuzzy, and friendly—and this Scotch ale is all of that.

A warm copper color gives forth to a biscuity nose that's filling in and of itself. The autumnal-hued frothy head is of an agreeable crunchiness. It's tart—almost winy—dry, strong, hoppy, bitter, assertive, long, complex, rich and well balanced. This beer would provide substance through the harshest rainy season. I've always been a little suspicious of any beer with a dog on the label, but this is one of Edinburgh's finest. Besides, Scotties are *nice* dogs.

BEERSTORY   MacAndrew's is brewed at the Caledonian Brewing Company, in Edinburgh. Caledonia operates the last remaining direct-fire copper kettles in Great Britain. Their beautiful brick brewery with its imposing smokestack is a fine example of Victorian industrial architecture.

The brewery was founded in 1864 and scheduled to be shut down in 1987. It was rescued by Russell Sharp, a former distiller for Chivas Regal.

For more on the Caledonian Brewing Company, see Caledonian Golden Pale.

FOOD RECOMMENDATIONS   Unless you've got a hankering for haggis—that traditional Scottish dish made of sheep hearts, liver, and offal—try this great Scotch ale with black bean soup, venison, roast turkey, lobster, rack of lamb, duck, hamburgers, aged cheddar and water biscuits, ham and Swiss sandwiches, melons, and pomegranates. Also makes a wonderful— if dizzifying—accompaniment to single malt Scotch whisky.

RECOMMENDED RELATED BEERS   Caledonian makes some great ales under the name Golden Promise. Try the organic Golden Promise Ale, the organic Golden Pale (pale ale), and the Double Dark (ale).

SPECIFICATIONS   I paid about $2.99 for a 17 oz. (500 ml) bottle of MacAndrew's Scotch Ale. The alcoholic content of MacAndrew's is 5.3 percent by weight, 6.5 percent by volume. MacAndrew's is brewed at The Caledonian Brewing Co., Slateford Road, Edinburgh EH11, 1PH, Scotland. Telephone: (031) 337 1286. The Caledonian Ale House is at 1-3 Haymarket Terrace, Edinburgh. Telephone: 01 31 337 1006. The beer is imported by Merchant du Vin, 140 Lakeside Avenue, Seattle, WA 98122-6538. Telephone: 206-322-5022. E-mail: info@mdv-beer.com.

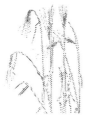

BEER NUMBER

50

Kwak
Brouwerie Boteels
Buggenhout, Dendermonde, Belgium

Silver Medal: Beverage Testing Institute, 1993

Try not to think of ducks when drinking Kwak. Besides it's made in Buggenhout. Buggenhout Kwak is the noise you'll make after a few of these. This is one strong beer, weighing in at 8 percent alcohol. This beer is orange and lively. The taste is virtually impossible to describe. It tastes of a Saturday morning flea market in the medieval center of Bruges, and of pretzels, pastry, smoked ham and oysters, whipped cream and pralines. It's got a slippery mouth feel that cleanses the palate while corrupting it with divine decadence. There are also hints of anise with an herbal nose.

BEERSTORY   Kwak has been called "the Coachman's Brew" for over 200 years. Pauwel Kwak, an enterprising Flemish stable owner and stagecoach innkeeper of the *Hoorne* (horn) on the post road between Malines and Ghent, began brewing this beer two years before Marie Antoinette lost her head in 1779. At the time, Napoleonic law stated that no stagecoach driver or postilion could drink with his passengers in a tavern. Not wanting to miss a sale, Kwak circumvented this law by selling his beer in a horn-shaped glass that could fit into a horse's stirrup and thus serve the coachmen out of doors. The strong but eminently drinkable amber beer from Buggenhout has been served in this unique glass since. You might recognize those glasses today as the three-foot-long "yard-of-ale" glasses available at some bars—complete with wooden stands to hold them upright.

Kwak eventually sold his brewery to the Bosteels family, and for the last six generations they have nurtured the business. When drinking outside the tavern fell out of fashion, the horn-shaped glass moved inside. By then the glass had become a collectable. So much so that Kwak patrons submitted to the custom of placing one shoe in a basket suspended over the bar to insure that the glass would be returned at the end of the night.

FOOD RECOMMENDATIONS   Crack a Kwak along with sturdy Flemish fare such as rabbit stew, roast chicken with frites (french fries), cheeses such as Gouda and Emmenthaler, or with salmon or swordfish. And who would deny Kwak with duck?

RECOMMENDED RELATED BEERS   There is only one Kwak.

SPECIFICATIONS   I paid $2.99 for an 11.2 oz. (330 ml) bottle of Kwak. The alcoholic content of Kwak is 8 percent by volume. Kwak is brewed at Brouwerij Bosteels, Kerkstr 92, B-9255 Buggenhout, Dendermonde, Belgium. Telephone: (052) 332282. It is imported by Vanberg & Dewulf, 52 Pioneer Street, Cooperstown, NY 13326. Telephone: 607-547-8184.

PART TWO

Everything I Need to Know I Learned From Beer

8

This Tut's for You:
A Brief History of Beer

I feel wonderful drinking beer; in a blissful mood, with joy in my heart and a happy liver.
—SUMERIAN POEM, 3,000 B.C.

Take a good look at the beer that (I hope) you're holding in your hand. Peer into the bubbles. Notice the color. Breathe deep the aroma. The color, the smell, the flavor, the *beer* is a little piece of ancient history brought forth to the modern world. If beer could talk it would tell tales of Babylonian princesses, Egyptian god-kings, and salty sailors. It would sing of Pilgrims, pirates, and outlaws. If your beer *did* talk, you'd probably be either very rich, crazy, or drunk.

Since your beer is (probably) not talking to you, it might interest you to know that the first brewers of beer were the ancient Babylonians. They first did it around 7,500 years ago. As civilization was dawning, folks with names like "Nog" and "Ur" were sitting around sipping barley brew out of clay pots with long, bamboo straws.

Some say "necessity is the mother of invention." But anyone familiar with food history is more likely to say "happy accidents make great comestibles." I doubt, for instance, that the first person to eat a jalpeño pepper did so after careful analysis and study. When they didn't die, they probably felt emboldened to try another.

So too with beer. What you had was your basic case of "whoops I left my sprouted barley out in the rain for a week." And Nog—looking at the foaming, heady brew—said, "Let's drink it!" After pushing aside the happily drowned flies, and maybe squeezing in some honey, Nog and Ur probably ended up chanting songs to the goddess all the live-long night.

While this is all speculation, what we do know is that by 1,800 B.C., the Sumerians were happily worshiping Ninkasi—the goddess of brewing, who was also called "the lady who fills the mouth." Ninkasi, incidentally, lived on the legendary Mount Sabu, whose name roughly translates as "mountain of the tavern keeper."

During this time the secrets to brewing beer were closely held by women. Men certainly *enjoyed* beer, but women were the keepers of the kettle flame. As a matter of fact, our previously mentioned Nog and Ur were probably women. It's more likely that women would have been working with barley grains in the first place. Cultural anthropologists—whose job it is to know these things—tell us that *all* religious myths in *all* ancient cultures say that beer was a gift *from the goddess to women.* It was never believed to be divinely granted to men. In those ancient cultures, dozens of goddesses were associated with beer, brewing, and drinking.

We must remember that life in the Tigris and Euphrates valley was no picnic back in the sixth-millennium B.C. There were the usual horrors of drought, disease, pestilence, and badly made sandals. On top of it all, people were forced to endure all this without any consciousness-altering libation. So, as you might imagine, when beer was discovered, it caught on quickly.

For the ancient Sumerians, the buzz of beer was considered a religious experience. Beer was thought to contain supernatural spirits that overtook the personality of the drinker. The sprites inspired the inebriated to great (or ridiculous) word and deed. And whatever was in it, our ancient ancestors wanted MORE!

The women who possessed the secrets of brewing were quickly elevated to priestesshood. Finding barley to make beer became an all-consuming task. Before long, the nomadic people of ancient Sumeria settled down in one place *so they could grow barley for the sole purpose of making beer.* Thus, city life was born. That may explain a few things about our cities today.

Clay pots and jugs that were left behind by the ancients are the principal record that we have today of those civilizations. Some anthropologists suggest that the pots and ceramics were invented solely for the purpose of holding beer. The brewsters needed something to put all that beer into. So the most telling records of our human past were basically antediluvian beer bottles. Of course, when scientists study our culture ten thousand years from now, they might wonder about all the brown bottles we left behind.

Be that as it may, once all the Babylonian brewsters—called Sabtiem—had a captive audience, it wasn't long before the tavern was born. Again, women ran the show. Besides brewing beer, women acted as tavern keepers, servers, staff, and even bouncers. Men didn't mess with the lady bouncers. The ladies had the spiritual protection of Siduri, who was the goddess of the brewery *and* the goddess of wisdom.

Images of bare-breasted women were carved into the walls of taverns in high relief, beckoning thirsty passersby. The drunken men sat and told tribal tales as the divine juice coursed through their veins. They ordered beer with names like "Black and White," "Beer of Sacrifice," and "Horned Beer."

In fact, there were dozens of beer styles to chose from. Besides the aforementioned black beer and white beer (*kurungig*), there was fine black beer (*kassag*), premium beer (*kassagasaan*), spiced beer (*kasusasig*), and a special "royal" beer called *kasnaglugal*. And lest you think that today's red-beer craze is anything new, the Babylonians also drank *kassig*, or red beer.

We'll never know if our ancient ancestors were aware that beer was damn good for them. The process of fermentation increased the vitamin and mineral value of barley fourfold. The wild yeasts that floated through the air—whose magic made the barley mash into beer—contained protein, vitamin B, and vitamin C. And those of us who drink home brew—or commercially made nonpasteurized beer—garner the same benefits today. As has been scientifically proven in the past few years, a couple of drinks a day helps prolong life and lower the risk of heart disease. Beer was also used as the base for most medicines and was thought to cure everything from boils to cancer to snakebites.

On top of it all, beer took a while to spoil. With its alcohol acting as a preservative, the nutritional values of beer lasted longer than any other foodstuff of the time. Throw in some herbs, date syrup, coconut, honey (with the comb), and wheat, and you've got a medicine that allowed you to talk to the spirits—and prevented disease and malnutrition. All in all, not too shabby for some barley left out in the rain.

In 1989, Fritz Maytag, owner of the Anchor Steam Brewery in San Francisco, brewed up a beer called Ninkasi. It was Maytag's attempt to duplicate a beer first brewed at the dawn of human history. The beer was a recreation of a Sumerian beer that was brewed around 2,800 B.C. The formula was gleaned from an ancient poem dedicated to Ninkasi that also contained the recipe for beer. The unhopped, honey-sweetened beer was brewed with half-baked barley loaves, called *bappir*, that could be eaten or thrown into water to make beer. Ninkasi was unveiled at the 1989 Microbrewers Convention and sold in the Bay Area for a few months.

While the Babylonians loved their brew, the Egyptians that followed them elevated beer to astounding new heights. The great pyramids and the Sphinx are engineering miracles. But almost every single living soul involved in their design and construction was drinking beer under the ancient Egyptian moonlight.

The folks of the pharaoh were obsessed with beer, which they called *hekt*. Their hieroglyph for food was a picture of a loaf of bread and a jug of beer. They anointed their newborns with the stuff. (Typical names for children of the time were "How Drunk Is Cheops," and "Hathor Is Besotted.") They filled the tombs of the dead with beer. And the salaried workers who built the pyramids were paid a minimum wage of four gallons of beer a day.

The Nile dwellers of long ago believed that beer was accidentally invented by the goddess Hathor, queen of drunkenness. The story goes that the Sun god Re was ticked off at the human race. He saw his temples fall to squalor and people doing the nasty out in public. Folks were lying, stealing, and sinning. Re sent Hathor to Earth to straighten out the Egyptian people.

Hathor came down in the form of a leopard and began to mop the streets with the miscreants. After one day, the streets were ankle-deep in blood and all the houses were flattened. Even Re thought this was a touch extreme. The trouble was, he had sent Hathor to Earth for three days and she could not be recalled before that time. Re needed to stop Hathor while he still had a few people left to worship him. That night Re came down to Earth in the form of a baboon and planted (what else?) barley in the blood in the streets, along with a few dates.

The barley quickly turned to beer in the next morning's sun. Hathor the leopard noticed the stuff and began to lap it up. Soon she was drunk on her back under a palm tree, snoozing. Two more days passed as the kitty from hell lay passed out. The humans were saved. For all their pain and suffering—as a consolation prize—they got beer. Hathor became the goddess of beer. A story with a happy ending.

The other reigning deity of beer was Menqut, the brewer goddess. Brewers were called *fty*, and the brewing process was called *th*. Egyptian brewers soaked half-baked loaves of barley bread in water for several days. Then they threw them in six-foot-tall vats and stomped them (maybe that's where the term *mash* came from). The *ftys* filtered the mash through tightly woven reed baskets into huge clay jars. The jars were sealed with mud from the Nile and the aging process began. The final product was flavored with cedar, honey, nutmeg, lavender, and other flowers.

Women in every home brewed beer. There were also several large commercial breweries that paid millions in excise taxes on the beer they made. The pharaohs employed chief beer inspectors to maintain quality control. And for his divine benevolence, the pharaoh received thousands of gallons of beer a year in the form of tax payments. One record from Egypt's Middle Kingdom—about 1,800 B.C.—shows that the royal court received 130 jars of beer *every day*. The queen herself rejoiced with five jars a day.

As in Sumeria, beer shops were common in the land of the pharaohs. Tavern patrons were offered plates full of a dried bitter herb called *skirret*. Drinkers placed a plug of the herb between the cheek and gum to give the sweet beer a bitter flavor.

As we all know, where there's beer, there are hangovers. The Egyptians called the malady "Pulling of the Hair." Their remedy? Cabbage juice. Don't laugh. Modern science has proved that cabbage juice contains chemicals that neutralize acetaldehydes, the nasty byproduct of our livers trying to metabolize alcohol.

Egyptian civilization eventually fell into decline. The arts of math, masonry, and malting were carried on without them. The Meso-Americans took the brewer's art to Central America.

The Greeks and the Romans called beer *cerevisia*. The word comes from the Roman goddess of agriculture Ceres and *vis*, which means "strength." The word *beer* comes from the Latin *bibere*, which means "to drink."

Once Rome fell, it would be almost a thousand years before anybody would be organized and centralized enough to brew beer on a large scale.

But the northern cultures kept the flame of the brewpot burning through the darkness of the early second millennia A.D.

SAINTS BE PRAISED!

Beer is mentioned frequently in the Talmud and in the Bible. Three of the rabbis that wrote the Talmud were brewers. David, king of the Jews, was a brewer. The shingle a brewery hung when it went into business was the six-pointed Star of David. The Star also represented alchemy—the turning of water into . . . beer.

The traveling traders of Mesopotamia carried the brewster's art north to Germany, Scandinavia, and the British Isles.

The Vikings carried ale as they carried on. They were ocean-crossing, tattooed, beer-crazed berserkers. A Viking's idea of a good time was to swill twenty ram's horns full of ale then rape, pillage, and burn. They raped Holland and England. They pillaged France and Italy. They burned Paris and Hamburg. And they kept huge casks of ale on board their ships for sustenance.

The word *ale* comes from the Viking *aul*. One of the reasons that Viking warriors were so fearless and downright crazy is that they brewed their ale with wormwood, a known madness-inducing hallucinogen.

The Vikings covered their drinking horns with magical runes. They had a litany of drunken, sadistic behavior that included getting their enemies dead drunk and burning down the pub with them in it. Then they celebrated by drinking ale from their boiled skulls.

Scotland was invaded by Vikings who were on their way to Iceland, Greenland, and Canada. The tiny, fairylike folk of Scotland were called Picts. They learned about tattooing and ale from the Vikes, presumably between bouts of rape and pillage. The Picts were ferocious warriors who had once driven back the Roman legions of Julius Caesar. The Picts threw Scottish heather into their ale. Not so coincidentally, heather leaves sometimes are covered with the ergot fungus—the base ingredient in LSD.

While beer-besotted fairy warriors were traipsing around Scotland, the brewing of beer was quickly becoming the stock-in-trade for priests, monks, and saints. In the early years of the first millennium, the holy men of the church were just about the only group of people organized enough to manage the complicated procedure of large-scale brewing from beginning to end.

Somewhere around A.D. 640, Arnou, the bishop of Metz died. Arnou's followers were carrying his body to its final resting place. Their grief was magnified when they ran out of beer. Somehow a magical goblet appeared that was the proverbial "bottomless cup" filled with beer. The townsfolk drank and drank, but—miraculously—the goblet never ran dry. Faster than you can say "canonization," Arnou was named the patron saint of brewers—the first of many.

When Charlemagne put together the Holy Roman Empire, he brought in Saint Gall to run his brewing bureaucracy. Gall had been trying to convert the pagan Celts. Instead they taught him the secret of ale brewing. Gall refined the process and soon the Holy Romans were brewing beer much as it is done in the modern age. With a saint like that, who needs sinners?

Soon the church was in control of all the beer. If you wanted beer, you had to pay your respects to the church. The abbots used the sweet reward of the pint to cajole the locals into coming to their rituals, ceremonies, and feasts. Thus was the term *church ale* invented for parties that commemorated the patron saints. Bride ales were parties in which a soon-to-be-married woman would disperse the suds in exchange for wedding gifts. Thus was the term *bridal* coined.

INNS, ALE HOUSES, AND DEADLY WATER

A quart of ale is a dish fit for a king.
—WILLIAM SHAKESPEARE

The nice thing about the church—they gave their ale away. To subsidize this fine tradition, they sold lesser quality potions to passing travelers. For six hundred years or so, it was well nigh impossible for an independent brewery to go into business. Who would pay money for what the church freely distributed? Of course, many an alewife made small batches for her family. Some sold their wares. But large-scale independent breweries were not viable until that happy little devil—known as the Black Plague of Europe—arrived in 1347.

Nothing shakes up the economy like the death of forty million people in four years. Entire towns and villages were left empty. Whatever wealth was around became concentrated in the hands of fewer people. This led to Europe's first consumer culture for the lucky survivors. By 1400 people were buying, selling, and traveling for business. They were also dressing up in silk and velvet. And nothing makes a person thirstier than power shopping.

Alewives soon found hoards of travelers lined up in their front rooms begging for accommodations and tankards of ale. The inn became the in spot to conduct business. As competition increased, innkeepers began to put shows, music, and balls in their barrooms. Like today's microbrewery boom, the number of inns increased exponentially. By the middle of the sixteenth century, there were almost twenty thousand inns where there had been only a handful one hundred years before.

Innkeepers not only supplied ale and a place to drink it, they provided lodging, entertainment, stables, and even warehouses for the traveling merchant's goods. By 1600 the innkeeper was generally the richest person in town.

Folks who didn't live the good life of the traveling merchant were usually relegated to establishments called taverns. Those on the bottom of the financial pecking order found themselves in what were called ale houses.

It was a good thing that the great unwashed also had something to drink and a place to drink it, because by the Middle Ages, the rivers, lakes, and streams of Europe were becoming nothing more than open sewers—the price of that consumer culture. The cry went up across the land: "Don't drink the water. Drink only beer!"

Where there's beer, there are bureaucrats. When the Magna Carta was written in 1215, it spelled out the liberties to be granted to the English people. It also contained a clause spelling out the standards for ale. This might have been more than necessary. By the fourteenth century there was one ale house or brew shop for every twenty-one people in London, whose growing population reached thirty-five thousand.

Like many hated government regulations, the precepts enacted by the Magna Carta grew out of true need. In the thirteenth century, sanitation was unheard of. One wag described ale thusly:

For muddy, foddy, fulsome, puddle stinking
for all of these, ale is the only drinking.

Another poet said ale would "make one cacke and spew" when describing the thick, mashy, low-alcohol, half-fermented product that many passed off as ale. The stuff was made variously from barley, wheat, oats, rice, millet, spelt, rye, wood chips, and sometimes onions and chicken entrails.

Enter the Germans. They were the first people on record, circa A.D. 750, to use hops in their brew. The hops balanced the sweetness of the malt, stabilized and preserved the brew, and had a medicinal effect. The Brits were appalled. They outlawed the use of hops in brewing and resisted the dreaded hop until the mid-1400s when Flemish and Dutch brewers began to import their hop-laden ales to the British Isles.

By the sixteenth century, German brewers were *verboten* to put anything in their beer besides hops, malted barley, malted wheat, and water. This law, known as the Reinheitsgebot was enacted in 1516 by the Bavarian King William VI.

Hops slowly caught on in southern England. Besides aiding flavor, they made it possible to brew ale in large batches and ship it throughout the Isles without spoilage. When ale was stored for longer periods, the solids in it settled, providing a clear, bitter beer. Fine British beer was born along with a new term. The unhopped, cloudy brew of old was defined in Samuel Johnson's first dictionary as "ale." The cleared, hopped brew was called "beer." After a while, however, the two terms became interchangeable.

With the new ability to brew large quantities and ship them about, breweries sprung up around pure water sources. The abbey at Burton-on-Trent was one of these early brewing centers. Before long, the pale ales of Burton found their way throughout the kingdom and even onto the Continent.

THE FIRST AMERICAN REVOLUTION IN BREWING

While all this brewing intrigue and progress was taking place in the towns and cities of Europe, half a world away lay the untamed wilderness that was America.

The folks who later became known as Pilgrims were not exactly suited to start a new nation in the wilderness. (They actually called themselves

Saints; the term *Pilgrim* was not given to them until two hundred years later.) These Saints were tailors, printers, merchants, shopkeepers, and hatters—not occupations you would associate with taming a continent. None of them knew how to hunt, that being a sport for the aristocracy of the time. They didn't even bring a fishing pole to the New World. But they did bring beer.

As a matter of fact, they were going to sail to a parcel of land near New York but they overshot their mark. They continued northward and finally landed at Plymouth because they ran out of beer. They had to disembark to make some more. Horror of horrors, the beer supply was so depleted that the Saints were forced to drink water! It practically caused a mutiny. Used to the stinking water sources of England, they didn't realize that the pure waters of the American wilderness were quite able to sustain them. The brewhouse was the first structure the Saints set about building. They would no more have voluntarily drunk water than eaten sand.

The tiny colony began to grow and so did beer consumption. When the Puritans arrived ten years later, they had three times more beer than water on board their ship. Malted barley was imported from England, and when supplies ran short they made a new American brew from a new American food source—maize. They also used pumpkins, parsnips, and walnut tree chips. These New World brews were flavored with sassafras and juniper berries.

By the end of the seventeenth century there were dozens of licensed commercial brewers in Boston and hundreds of unlicensed ones. Sailors—who believed drinking water would kill a man—loaded their boats with dozens of barrels of beer before sailing across the ocean blue. Ship's captains supplemented their income by investing in breweries.

Harvard University had its own brewhouse, and the college was shut down by a general strike at one point by students protesting the shortage of beer. Other colleges similarly had their own brewhouses for students and faculty.

The 1700s were a heady time for the new nation. Craftsmen and laborers expected beer as part of the compensation for their labors.

> Ben Franklin wrote of a friend who worked in his print shop who had a "pint before breakfast, a pint with breakfast with his bread and cheese, a pint between breakfast and dinner, a pint with dinner, a pint in the afternoon, about six o'clock, and another when his day's work was done."

Ale was drunk out of black leather mugs, called "blackjacks." There were four main styles of beer: Small beer was the weakest, enjoyed at home, even by small children. Ship's beer was next in strength, followed by table beer. Strong beer was at the top of the list, and in the later years, dark, roasty porter became very popular.

The fledgling colonial government used taverns as courthouses as circuit judges rode from one town to another to grease the wheels of justice.

As could be expected, there were people who resented spending their days in the company of hundreds of drunken sots. Periodically, judges and governors enacted laws like the 1712 "Act Against Intemperance, Immorality, and Prophaneness and the Reformation of Manners." Needless to say, these laws were by and large ignored. But other things were taking place in pubs besides drinking. There was also the heated talk of politics that got the Crown and its minions nervous. Before long, the government tried to limit each town—with the exception of ports—to only one tavern. That really gave the colonists something to complain about.

After losing a war with France in 1764, the Brits imposed a heavy excise tax on imported beer. Soon the Crown had a full-scale revolution on its hands. Americans refused to drink beer imported from England, which further fueled the colonial brewing industry. As the English added more items to the tax roles, a full-fledged revolution was organized in taverns over blackjacks of ale. The angry colonists organized a boycott of British goods, including beer.

The list of famous eighteenth-century beer lovers is a long one. Samuel Adams organized the Boston Tea Party over tankards of ale in the Green Dragon Tavern. John Hancock was supplied with thirty gallons of beer a month from a local brewer during the Revolutionary War.

George Washington's expense account included scores of entries for a drink called *flip* that was made from beer, rum, cream, sugar, and eggs. Really. The pièce de résistance in flip preparation was when a red-hot poker was taken from the fireplace and plunged into the gooey drink, expelling foam all over the table and drinker alike. (Not a picture of Washington you're likely to see in the history books.) Making sure to supply his soldiers with plenty of fresh beer in the field, General Washington managed to forge a new nation under ale. After the framers of the Constitution finished their immortal task, Washington wrote, "the business being closed, the members adjourned to the City Tavern."

OUT WITH THE ALE, IN WITH THE LAGER

The nation may have been born of beer, but by the 1800s it was fueled by rum. President Thomas Jefferson lamented that nearly a third of his countrymen died from dancing with demon rum. Jefferson longed for the bygone days of beer's prominence in American culture. To resolve the problem, the president invited master brewers from Bohemia to school brewers in the United States. Jefferson's wife, Martha, designed a brewery at the Monticello estate and began producing beer there in 1813. She seasoned it with hops that she had traded for "an old shirt."

Jefferson's concern over booze quickly became the battleground for the first organized American temperance movement. Fervor-crazed New England farmers took to their apple orchards with axes so that no evil cider could be brewed. This was actually beneficial to the brewers of beer, a drink that even the abolitionists, considered something of a tonic.

> In spite of the prohibitionists, America continued to drink. And in great amounts. One English naval officer observed: "Americans can fix nothing without a drink. If you meet you drink, if you part you drink . . . if you close a bargain you drink . . . they drink because it's hot, they drink because it's cold; they begin to drink early in the morning, they leave off late at night; they commence it early in life and continue until they soon drop off dead. As for water, it's very good for navigation."

Mathew Vassar became the first wealthy national brewer, selling the likes of *Poughkeepsie Do and Ale*. Vassar's breweries produced thirty thousand barrels a year at a time when the brewer's year was seasonal, lasting from September to April. Vassar took his considerable brewing fortune and started the first American college for women, Vassar College, in 1861.

By the second decade of the 1800s, thousands of German immigrants began pouring into the United States. Wisconsin and Missouri were favorite destinations of the Germans, along with Philadelphia, Cincinnati, and Chicago. And of course the Germans did not leave their beer-loving ways in the old country. According to historian Samuel Elliot Morison, "the German didn't give up his beer, instead, he made Milwaukee famous."

The new Americans also introduced new beer styles to an English menu dominated by porters, bitters, and stouts. The Germans brought with them bock, weisse, and alt. This quickly ingratiated the Germans to the American natives, who were glad to have such skilled brewers in their towns and cities.

Two new inventions combined to change the beer-drinking habits of Americans forever. One was the clipper ship, the fastest sailing vessel ever built at the time. These boats shortened the trip across "the pond" so much so that beer could now weather the trans-Atlantic journey. Import beer became a hot item. While clipper ships may have faded into history, another invention from that time is still with us—lager beer. It was an immediate sensation.

Lager beer is brewed with bottom-fermenting yeast at cold temperatures. The style originated in Bavaria, where beer was *lagered*, or stored, in caves for up to six months at temperatures approaching freezing. This gives the particulates in the beer a chance to settle, thereby making a clean, clear brew. Ale by comparison is top-fermented and drunk within a few weeks of brewing.

By the mid-1800s millions of Americans had dispensed with heavy pewter, clay, and wood tankards, which hid the cloudy, dark ale from the eye of the drinker. Instead, crystal-clear glasses full of light, sparkling lager were the order of the day. The first lager brewery went into business in Philadelphia in 1840. Around that same time, the Adam Lemp family of St. Louis became the first national lager brewer.

In 1842 another milestone in brewing occurred when a brewery in Pilsen, Bohemia, produced the world's first golden lager. Now part of the Czech Republic, the soft water and noble hops of the Pilsen region combined to make pilsner-style beer one of the first styles to sweep across Europe and America, knocking quite a few other styles off the charts. Before long the words *pilsner*, *pils*, and *pilsener* were popping up on hundreds of American beer bottles, along with the term *Bohemian style*.

This beer boom also fueled a burgeoning hop business. From New York to Wisconsin, hop farms were shooting up as fast as their vines would carry them.

In 1860, America's breweries produced one million thirty-one-gallon barrels of beer. In 1867 they produced six million barrels at about 1,300 breweries from coast to coast.

Refrigeration was invented in 1869, and the technique was seized immediately by brewers who began to manufacture lager beer all year long. Other improvements in brewing technology allowed for an uninterrupted flow of mass-produced beer for the first time in history. By the eighth decade of the 1800s, one production record after another fell by the wayside as America's 2,300 brewers fueled beerhalls full of new immigrants flooding into the country. Like all revolutions, however, this one was not without casualties. Some of America's venerable old ale breweries shut their doors forever. But until the twentieth century, English ales and European lagers existed side by side in America, something that was unique in the world until the *second* brewing revolution that is in progress today.

During the nineteenth century, the population of America grew fourfold. Its transportation system went from horse and cart on rutted paths to gleaming coast-to-coast railroads. Cities like New York introduced reservoir systems that supplied the city (and its brewers) with a constant supply of fresh water. German and Czech immigrants brought sophisticated brewing technology, which was amplified by inventions undreamed of before. As the century closed there were ninety-four breweries in Philadelphia alone. There were seventy-seven in Manhattan, thirty-eight in Brooklyn, forty-one in Chicago, twenty-four in Cincinnati, thirty-three in Detroit, twenty in Buffalo, twenty-nine in St. Louis, and twenty-six in San Francisco. The thirsty new Americans created an explosion in brewing that brought a king's ransom to those fortunate enough to participate in it.

THE GOLDEN AGE OF BREWING MEETS THE BLIND PIG

Oh, how the money rolled in! Breweries whose names we still recognize today were each producing up to half a million barrels a year. Pabst, Blatz, Anheuser-Busch, Miller, Schlitz and others were not simply neighborhood breweries. As the big breweries increased their marked share, unique styles and regional brands fell by the wayside, and one result of this was that the seventy-seven breweries in New York in 1890 had shrunk to only thirty-seven by 1910. As it became harder and harder to find dunkles and porters, another monster crept into the American biergarten that would change the way the country drank for the next seventy years.

The idea of alcohol prohibition was not new in 1919. Laws calling for the "suppression of Drinking houses and Tippling shops" were first passed in Maine in 1851. Minnesota, Rhode Island, Massachusetts, Vermont,

Michigan, Connecticut, New York, New Hampshire, and others soon followed suit. These laws were famously ignored.

After Maine's first prohibition law went into effect, entrepreneurs ran ads in the paper inviting people to come view a "blind pig" for a small admission. The Blind Pigs always included free beer, and usually a drunken pig.

Prohibition returned with a vengeance when the Women's Christian Temperance Union was formed in Ohio in 1874. The temperance movement developed strong footholds in rural areas with strong religious movements. Before long, the six-foot-tall Carrie Nation was busting up barrooms with an ax and at the same time gathering plenty of free publicity for the antidrinking movement.

As the horrors of World War I were becoming clear to the nation, the "drys" seized the anti-German hysteria to further their cause. In 1917, drawing on a hatred of all things German, Congress gave President Woodrow Wilson war powers under the Food Control Act that allowed him to prohibit the manufacture of beer. Soon a Constitutional Amendment was proposed. Prohibition, in the form of the Volsted Act, was ratified by thirty-six states in January 1919, and alcoholic beverages were banned from the United States.

As we all know, Prohibition didn't work. Ironically it affected beer—the drink of moderation—much more than it affected demon rum or bathtub gin, which was concentrated and therefore easier to smuggle, hide, and consume. As America's great brewing institutions shut their doors, stills producing "white lightning" sprang up on hills and in dales across the country.

Professional brewers were shocked and stunned. Some tried to get by making soda, ice cream, and near beer. But as one wag stated: "Whoever called it near beer was a poor judge of distance!" Schlitz made chocolate. Coors made malted milk. Blatz made industrial alcohol. Grocers sold malt syrup with hops and yeast in a bucket that a patient home brewer could turn into serviceable beer. The concoction came with explicit instructions of what *not* to do, like add water and leave in the basement, lest the stuff turn—horror of horrors—into beer. Some grocers sold over two thousand pounds of malt syrup a day as over 177,000 speakeasies opened their doors.

Then the Great Depression hit. People lost their homes, their jobs, and their families. To make matters worse, they couldn't even get a decent beer. Franklin Roosevelt could have won the presidency simply for his call to end Prohibition. On April 7, 1933, beer once again gushed forth. A grateful America consumed over one million gallons of beer that night. But the burden was great on the remaining brewers. Of the sixteen hundred pre-Prohibition brewers, only seven hundred reopened. With little capital, and old, obsolete equipment, five hundred of those folded before long.

At Prohibition's end, most Americans under the age of thirty had never tasted a real beer. The remaining large brewers spent millions of dollars in advertising to convince America that yellow, soda-poppy low-hopped lager was the way beer was *supposed* to taste. Who knew better?

After World War II, most of America became a homogenized country. The wonders of white bread, processed cheese, and canned meat followed white America into the blooming suburbs. Beer was Kool-Aid with a kick. You drank it in a gulp and threw the can out the window of your chopped and channeled '51 Mercury.

Many older breweries with aging equipment did not latch on to the prosperity that skyrocketed across the American economy. In Europe thousands of breweries were destroyed during the war. As the world tuned into prepackaged TV, old breweries and their great styles fell flatter than a barley pop on an August afternoon. One by one, great beer styles pooped out to the pee-yellow, overcarbonated American pilsner monster.

In the merger mania of the 1980s, big brewers gobbled up little ones like so many fish in the ocean. Overleveraged and in a flat market, many of these megabreweries began to sink because of their overfull bellies. Into this milieu a few post-sixties revolutionaries stepped to the fore.

9

Free at Last: The Fermentation of Independence

THE ROOTS OF REAL ALE

It's true that the big, ugly business mergers began in the '80s—the 1880s. Even back then, it made good business sense to buy up the brewing competition, keep their label and name, and fill their bottles with your beer.

However, the great progress and discoveries of the twentieth century pushed every aspect of life further and further away from the traditional—and some say better—methods of old. In the world of brewing, quality, tradition, and craft gave way to modern, soulless factories where the bottom line mattered more than the beer. By the 1960s, brewers were modernizing production methods even in Great Britain—a country known for lovingly preserving its past. The British tradition was to serve up unfiltered cask-conditioned beer—that is, beer whose carbonation was developed naturally in the barrel with live yeast. Modernization found more and more breweries serving pasteurized and filtered ale. Since pasteurizing kills living yeast, brewers had to inject their beer artificially with carbon dioxide. It was cheaper to make and easier to serve.

In 1971 a group of folks could stand it no longer. They started a campaign to save *real* ale, and the Campaign for Real Ale (CAMRA) was born. Started out of a desire to preserve great beer for themselves, it soon became a nationwide consumer movement. CAMRA began to publish a newsletter called *What's Brewing?* They also published a book called the *Good Beer Guide*, identifying pubs that served cask-conditioned ale. (Both the newspaper and the updated book are still in publication. See appendix F for CAMRA's address.)

CAMRA struck a nerve with the British public, and soon the art of brewing and beer drinking was noticed by Britain's respected press. CAMRA began to sponsor the Great British Beer Festival in different cities each August. Nowadays attendance runs upward of fifty thousand attendees.

CAMRA has over twenty-five thousand card-carrying members. Whenever a brewery faces extinction or takeover, CAMRA demonstrators appear with a marching band, horse-drawn carriages, and coffins bearing beer barrels and mugs. Of course the media loves a good story, and CAMRA demonstrations have garnered national press coverage in Britain. Many a brewery has been saved from doom by the dedicated CAMRA operators. Today CAMRA has become a national clearinghouse for beer quality, legislation, price, and so forth.

The idea behind CAMRA caught on in Belgium, Scandinavia, Canada, and the Netherlands. They inspired many Americans and can take credit for restoring interest in real ale in the United States. Everything from their newsletters to their beer festivals have been imitated and improved on with great success.

By the 1980s the production of beer in America was in the control of so few hands that it started to look as if there would soon be only three or four breweries left. But something was happening simultaneously all over the world that would strike like lightning and fire a thousand brewing kettles.

The cold war had been funneling millions of baby boomers to Great Britain and Europe for years. In the early seventies, the dollar was at an all-time high against European currencies. This initiated a travel craze among boomers looking to "discover" Europe. Once there, they couldn't help but find the cornucopia of delicious beer styles that had been forgotten in American since their great-grandfathers were alive. When the boomers returned to home shores, they still found a few of their favorite Euro-beers, but the flavor had been desiccated by time and travel—it just wasn't as good in Des Moines as it was in Düsseldorf.

While all this was going on, the post-sixties craze for healthy, pure foods became faddish—especially in California. Obscure little wine companies in Northern California suddenly had carloads of devotees clogging their country lanes every weekend. After growing up on cola in the car and instant coffee crystals in a cup, people suddenly discovered that here was a beverage that could be swirled, sipped, and slowly savored. A drink that needed time, patience, and skill to produce? What a relief! Americans were actually developing sophisticated palates worthy of their European cousins.

But good wine ain't cheap. People figured if Mr. Gallo could make it, so could they. Wine supply stores popped up and the back-to-the-land types were soon swilling out of five-gallon glass carboys in their basements.

At the same time, American beer lovers were beginning to demand better. Smaller regional breweries made a few decent beers, but many were falling to the big guys. European beer sold in America was mostly "dumbed down" to satisfy the prototypical American taste as the Euro-brewers saw it.

Scrappy Americans began to brew their own. This trend accelerated when President Jimmy Carter legalized home brewing in 1976. (It seems when Prohibition was repealed, home wine-making was legalized, but they forgot to mention beer.) Wine supply stores began to carry malt, hops, yeast, and brewing equipment.

People bought home-brew kits and turned their kitchens into beer laboratories. When the brew turned out better than Bud, they were hooked. Once you've gone bock, you never go back. After a few home brews, friends and neighbors usually commented: "You should start your own brewery!" A few of them were just drunk enough to try.

Americans are capitalists. Thomas Edison started out as an eccentric tinkerer in his garage and ended up as one of the wealthiest men in the world. Just as brewers from the beginning of time realized, people are thirsty. Brew it and they will drink.

BREWING ON THE FRITZ

Sometimes with hindsight, history looks less like accident and more like destiny. Take the story of Fritz Maytag. Born Francis Louis Maytag III, in Amana, Iowa, Fritz pretty much had it all. His family had become famous with a herd of prize-winning livestock. They invented Maytag blue cheese—a much-loved style. Later they made a fortune in the washing machine and refrigerator business. The Maytag repairman might have been lonely, but Fritz was expected to go to college and run his family's appliance empire. But beer intervened.

Fritz was sitting in a bar in San Francisco in 1965 enjoying his favorite beer—Anchor Steam, made by Anchor Brewing. Anchor had been born in 1869 and was the last of 150 steam breweries that once populated California and the Pacific Northwest.

Steam beer was a product of West Coast ingenuity, invented in the Gold Rush of 1849. There was no ice or refrigeration in San Francisco in those days, so brewers needed a way to satisfy the demands of the miners looking for gold in them thar hills. The brewers used a lager yeast—in which beer is fermented at very cold temperatures. But they made the beer at ale temperatures—around 60 degrees Fahrenheit—right about the average San Francisco summer's day. This new product was called steam beer.

By the 1930s, Anchor was the only steam brewery left in the world. They sold only keg beer to bars and restaurants locally. The brewery limped along for years with outmoded equipment and no bottling line. When Maytag, who was attending Stanford University, heard that Anchor was going out of business "tomorrow," he visited the brewery. Before the day was over, Fritz laid down $5,000 for the last steam beer brewery.

By 1971, Anchor Steam was producing an all-malt steam beer and bottling on premise. Next came a porter. Anchor turned its first profit in 1975. For the Bicentennial in 1976, Anchor brought out Liberty Ale. Later came Old Foghorn, a barley wine. In 1977, Anchor began work on a new brewery on Mariposa Street. Profits soon doubled. In twelve years, Anchor went from producing six hundred barrels of beer a year to eighty-two thousand barrels. And it's still growing.

Maytag made history by brewing porter and barley wine again in America—in a place where people would appreciate it. The effect was mercurial on West Coast beer devotees. While hundreds of post-sixties revolutionary ideas were spilling out of San Francisco (from rock 'n' roll to women's liberation), under the radar screens of the megabrewers, a revolution was fomenting with every sip of Liberty Ale and Old Foghorn that was consumed.

THE FIRST MICROBREWERY

It was a little easier for Fritz Maytag than for most. After all, he bought a working brewery and had the funds to realize his dream. But the story of America's first post-Prohibition *microbrewery* is another story entirely. Half a world away from Fritz and the Bay, Jack McAuliffe was a young technician at a U.S. naval base in Scotland. Between shifts maintaining Polaris "Boomer" submarines, Jack was maintaining his sanity through the cold, wet Scottish winters sampling real ale at the local pubs. The rich flavors and higher gravities of the ales intrigued him.

Jack returned to Sonoma, California, in 1973, but he couldn't find a beer worth drinking. Jack figured "why do without when I can do it myself." With the barest hint of brewing knowledge and very little money, Jack began scrounging pipes, army surplus, and old dairy equipment.

If he would have tried to call a beer equipment manufacturer, they would have laughed him off the phone. In 1973 only giant breweries bought giant brewing equipment. There was no such thing as a small, turnkey brewing system. (Thank goodness those days are over.)

Jack slapped together his minibrewing system in a rented warehouse leased to him by a local fruit company. Jack put his government-taught skills to work and began welding, wiring, and brewing. He hired a schooled, professional brewing scientist named Don Barkley. With stainless steel open tanks used for dairy production, Jack and Don began brewing New Albion Ale, so named to honor the ancient moniker of England—Albion.

The first year, New Albion brewed about 150 thirty-one-gallon barrels and resurrected a few nearly extinct styles. Jack struggled along for about six years. His space was too small to meet demand, his advertising almost nonexistent. Interest rates in the late seventies were about 20 percent. All these things conspired to New Albion's demise in 1982. But Jack's brewing equipment went on to complete many years of dedicated service at Medicino Brewing Company in the appropriately named town of Hopland, California. Before long, dozens of folks who had seen Jack's microbrewery began snatching up used equipment from puzzled dairy farmers. From such circumstances was a brewing rebellion born.

Before long, microbreweries were bubbling up from coast to coast. A few of the notable early starters were Sierra Brewing Company in Chico,

California, which opened in 1981 to brew Sierra Nevada beer. Another upstart was the Boston Beer Company, makers of Samuel Adams beer, which opened for business in 1984. Today there are over 215 microbreweries in the United States and 40 in Canada, with about 60 new micros expected to open every year into the foreseeable future. Taxable production of microbreweries is growing at an astounding 50 percent a year. Now that's good news!

HOMEMADE BEER AND GOOD EATS

The guys who started minibreweries had rough times—some still do. First of all, they were trying to sell English-style ales to an American public weaned on bubbly American lagers. Plus, the English drink ninety percent of their ales in the pub; the Americans drink ninety percent of their lagers at home. This meant bottling for the microbrewers if they wanted to be competitive. Putting beer in a bottle and keeping it drinkable for weeks afterward is an entirely different science from brewing. And bottling lines are expensive. Thousands took the challenge, though, and got us where we are today.

Still, there's nothing like a great pub. And better yet, there's nothing like a great pub that brews its beer right there in the bar—a brewpub. This tradition goes back to ancient Sumeria, the Europeans perfected the art, and America had its share of brewpubs before Prohibition.

The first brewpub to open in America after Prohibition was the aforementioned Mendocino Brewing Company. But they only beat one of the more inspirational figures in the brewpub mythology by a few weeks. Buffalo Bill Owens, like many, studied beer in college between classes. While in college, Bill began home brewing on his own eccentric system. Like many before him, Bill traveled to Europe, where he learned what *real* beer tasted like.

Upon his return to the Bay Area, Bill became an award-winning photographer, working for national magazines like *Newsweek.* In the early seventies his photo book *Suburbia* was a popular seller with photos of various eccentrics living in California's booming suburbs. While Bill was teaching night courses in photography at an adult-education school, he noticed a class with even more students than his own. The packed classrooms were teaching home beer brewing.

Recognizing a trend when he saw one, Bill soon began to agitate the California state legislature to change its antiquated "three-tier" beer law that did not allow an alcohol manufacturer to sell directly to the public. Proving you can fight city hall and win, Californians were soon allowed to sell directly to the public in a restaurant setting.

While the wheels of law ground steadily on, Bill designed his brewpub in the Bay Area town of Hayward. When the revised brewpub law went into effect in September 1983, Bill opened the taps. Since that time, 365 brewpubs have opened in the United States and another 60 or so in Canada. About 100 are expected to open every year from now on.

Bill also revived one of the more interesting beer styles to come out of the craft-brewing movement—Pumpkin Ale. Based on a recipe from the time of George Washington, Pumpkin Ale is an incredible taste treat. Bill's other famous brew is Alimony Ale: the Bitterest Beer in America. Both beers are contract brewed and may be found in bottle shops across the land.

So we have come full circle. We may not be back to the brewery numbers before Prohibition, but we're getting there. And in today's vicious political and business climate, that's a miracle.

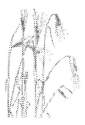

Appendix A

Ease-Hops Fables: Beer Ingredients

I mentioned earlier Bavarian King William VI's law, called the Rein-heitsgebot, which put the official stamp on what everybody already knew: beer should be made from barley. This law was essential because unscrupulous brewers used everything imaginable to make beer, including spelt, coarse sugar, tree bark, parsnips, onions, and even dead chickens. Like beer-loving Bavaria, England too eventually passed beer purity laws—though not as stern as the Reinheitsgebot's.

In England, an army of inspectors was hired to make sure people were getting good beer. One of the ways they determined the maltiness of a beer was to pour some on a chair, sit on it, and see if their pants stuck. The density and gravity of the beer was then taxed accordingly. Unfortunately, America never had a law like the Reinheitsgebot.

That said, here's a little refresher course on beer's ingredients so you can further enjoy the taste of what you're getting when you pop the top of a great one.

MALTED BARLEY

Malt is the basic ingredient of beer and it gives beer its flavor. Mixed with yeast, the sugars in malt give beer alcohol and carbonation. Malt is barley that has been sprouted in water and exposed to high temperatures at the moment of germination. The length and heat of those temperatures determine the color and characteristics of the malt and, later, the beer. Specialty malts are used to give beer unique flavors, from caramel to roasted coffee. Other specialty malts give beer its color, from straw to copper-red to deep brown and black.

Malted barley *is* beer. It is to beer what the Mona Lisa is to paintings. Malt is the powerful foundation that everything following it is built upon. The style and quality of malt infuses the drink with body, flavor, tone, and color. When properly nuanced by the brewer, barley can add the passion, texture, and physical attraction of a great painting. It's powerful stuff, and it's been around for a long, long time.

Barley first grew wild in the ancient hills of Sumeria for more than a million years. It is a member of the grass family, and its kernels are technically the fruit of the grass plant. Barley was first domesticated and worshiped as a goddess in the highlands of Levant about one thousand centuries ago. At that time, the great goddess barley was enticing people to give up their nomadic ways and settle down to cultivate her. They did it for beer. By the time Sumeria was established as the first civilization, over 40 percent of their barley crop was used for beer.

That the ancients had beer at all is a miracle that might be attributed to the gods and goddesses. Extracting the sugary juices of barley is a complicated procedure. First the barley must be steeped in water for forty-eight hours, until it softens. Then it has to be rinsed and kept moist while it germinates for a week. Right before the kernel sprouts, the "green malt," as it is called, has to be hauled off to kilns to dry. The barley is heated from 122 degrees Fahrenheit to 450 degrees Fahrenheit for thirty-five to forty hours. Then it is called malt.

When it is malted, the grain changes colors. It may be whitish-tan to dark brown or black. It also develops enzymes that are necessary for fermentation.

In the old days, this complicated procedure was done in various ways. A farmer might chuck a sack of barley in the river for a few days and dry it on the floor of his attic using shuttered gables that would allow the wind to blow over the grain. The grain might have been malted on a sieve over a crackling alder or peat fire. This would give the beer a delicious smoky flavor that may still be savored in today's *rauchbiers*.

As the years advanced, wood and peat were replaced by indirect coke fires. Barley might have been kilned while spread out on huge stone floors and carefully raked to prevent mold. Or it might have been roasted in drums like coffee roasters.

After Prohibition ended, the trend in America was toward light-bodied, light-flavored "American pilsners." All this "liteness" was achieved by brewers using unmalted corn and rice as an adjunct to barley. The adjuncts were readily available, cheap, easy, and apparently no one knew the difference.

Today the tide has turned. Tiny little microbreweries proudly boast on their labels that their beer is all malt and brewed in accordance with the Reinheitsgebot. The big bad brewers have had to take notice. Let's face it, beer brewed any other way isn't really beer, and most corn-laden hybrids taste vaguely like old chicken feed. Some great specialty beers use candy sugar, oats, or even pumpkins in their beer to give them a unique taste. But in general, beer is basically a barley-based beverage.

Brewers can be very particular about their barley. Some feel that great lagers can be made only from barley sown in spring, as it has the soft, clean flavors that German and Czech brewers in particular seek. Ale brewers, most notably the English and Belgians, desire barley sown in winter, as it gives their drink a hardy, vigorous edge.

Then there's the matter of rows. Two-row barley has two rows of grain on each ear. It grows in cooler climates and is more expensive to farm. Six-row barley has six rows of grain per ear and yields the most fermentable sugars per acre. Naturally big brewers prefer the cheaper six-row, which gives the beer a slightly husky taste. Two-row barley is the choice of quality brewers everywhere, whether they be American microbrewers or European brewers in general.

Some original "heritage" strains of quality barley are becoming more difficult to find, as tradition and flavor is further eroded in favor of commerce and efficiency.

The length that a malt is kilned will directly affect the flavor of the beer. Pilsner malts are treated the gentlest and have a golden color and a sweet, clean malt flavor. English two-row is a classic pale ale malt that is kilned longer to give it a little more color and a biscuitlike flavor. German specialty malts such as Munich malt are kilned even longer for a more copper color and a hint of pretzel flavor.

Specialty malts add more flavor and color to beer. Crystal malt is caramelized to give beer a caramel flavor. Deep-roasted malts are heated to the point of carbonization and may be chocolate or black in color. They give beer a dark color and a roasted or coffeelike flavor.

The lightest beers may be made from only one kind of light malt.

Some porters may contain as many as eight different types of malt. Brewers blend malt like a painter blends paint or a chef combines ingredients to produce a masterpiece of noticeable complexity.

Here are some types of malt and their characteristics as rated from lightest to darkest:

Lager malt is a two-row variety used in most lager-beer styles. It is light in color and has a cereal flavor. It's the basic ingredient of lager beers.

Wheat malt is made from wheat. It's light in color and gives the beer a thick mouth feel and strong head along with a clovelike flavor. Malted wheat is used in weizen, weisse, and some Belgian beers.

Pale ale malt is a two-row used in ales and imparts a biscuity, toasted flavor with just a hint of toffee.

Caramel malt is a specialty malt that is roasted at 300 degrees Fahrenheit. It gives the beer a sweet flavor and a slightly red hue.

Crystal malt is a sweet caramel-flavored malt that gives beer a ruby-red hue and a rich, sweet flavor. It is used in lagers, exports, and red, or amber-style, beers.

Brown malt gives beer a warm, baked flavor and a golden-brown color. Traditionally, brown malt was roasted over ash, hazel, and birchwood fires. Brown malts are somewhat rare and used mainly to produce "winter warmers."

Chocolate malt is named for its color not its flavor. Chocolate malt gives beer a coffee, caramel, and burnt flavor along with a dark, chocolatey color. It gives beer a roasted "bite." Chocolate malt is used in brown ales, stouts, and porters.

Black malt was once called Black Patent, an English trade name for the patented process. Black malt is darker than chocolate and gives sweet stouts and dark beers a sharp, acrid flavor and black color.

Roasted barley is used almost exclusively in Irish stouts like Murphy's and Guinness. It is stronger, drier, and more bitter than black malt and is characterized by the flavor of burnt coffee and an pleasantly acrid aftertaste. Roast barley also imparts the rich, creamy head associated with Guinness, Murphy's Irish Stout, and others.

Brewers have to combine science and art to blend malt in every batch of beer they brew. They chew the malt to decipher its flavor. They assess the moisture in the grain with laboratory instruments or plain native knowledge. They grind the malt to specific densities to compensate for its other qualities. In the end, it's the quality and handling of the malt that synthesizes plain water into an elixir worthy of the praise of gods and mortals alike.

Hops

Hops are the cone-shaped flowers of the hop plant, *humulus lupulus*. They are savored for their bittering and flavoring qualities, which preserve beer and give it its bouquet. Hops have been used in beer since at least A.D. 800. Tannins in hops help preserve beer. Hops grown in different regions are valued for their different qualities, whether bitter, floral, or flavorful.

It's no accident that the main ingredient used to perfume beer—the hop flower—is first cousin to cannabis sativa: marijuana. The two possess similar aromatic idiosyncrasies and both have a calming—even sleep-inducing—effect on the human body. Both of their flowers leave a gooey residue on the fingers that is difficult to rinse off.

The first written reference to hop use in beer comes from a German Benedictine nun called Hildegarde who lived from 1198 to 1179. (Her writings also mention cannabis as a cure for headaches.) Early hop references can also be found in Bohemia, northern France, and Flanders. Hops reached Britain in the fifteenth century and caused quite a scandal before they were accepted decades later.

Hops are a perennial crop. Modern hopyards contain twenty-foot poles, resembling telephone poles, that are spaced about every twenty feet. A strong wire runs across the top of the poles. From that wire single wires run down to each hop plant. As summer progresses, the hops snake their way up their wires. By the end of the growing season, each wire contains a lush pyramid-shaped hop plant in all its glory. In the heat of August, a hop vine can grow as much as two feet *a day*.

When the hops are ripe they are harvested by machinery and dried at 160 degrees Fahrenheit for about nine hours. They are cooled and compressed into two-hundred-pound bales and shipped to warehouses where they are cool-stored.

The rich, volcanic soil of the Pacific Northwest makes it a perfect place to grow hops. Almost all the commercial hops grown in North

America are grown in the Yakima Valley in Washington State, the Willamette Valley in Oregon, the Snake River Valley in Idaho, and in British Columbia, Canada. The United States grows twenty-five percent of the hops in the world, whereas Germany grows thirty percent.

Some types of hops are grown for their bouquet, some are grown for their bittering and preserving qualities. Here are a few of the most famous hop varieties and where they are grown.

Saaz hops are grown in Zatac, Bohemia, and valued for their floral qualities that give real pilsner its gorgeous bouquet.

Hallertau hops are grown in the Bavarian district of the same name. They are the favored aroma hop for German lagers.

Tettnang hops are similar to Hallertau and grown in the Baden-Württemberg area of Bavaria.

Northern brewer is a very bitter hop grown in Great Britain.

Goldings and *Fuggles* are the hops that give British ales their famous bouquet and bitterness. Both are named after the farmers who propagated them in the seventeenth and eighteenth centuries, respectively.

Cascade hops are grown in the Pacific Northwest. Cascade hops give American microbrews the floral quality that sets Euro-brewer's teeth on edge. American brewers are generally hop heads who would use twice as many of the bitter flowers if the public would let them. I can smell the Olympic rain forests in Cascade hops along with piney, floral, fruity, and citric notes.

Hops are blended with differing percentages of bitter and floral ingredients to give each beer its own unique characteristics.

Brewers use hops in three different forms—whole flowers, compressed pellets, and extracts. Whole flowers are a messy proposition to filter from the beer, but in my opinion the best for bouquet. Pellets are vacuum packed and common enough in many breweries. Hop extracts do no justice to the beer. Some brewers use a combination of flowers, pellets, and extract.

YEAST

Yeast is a single-celled fungus that eats sugar and multiplies rapidly. The byproduct of this action is carbon dioxide and alcohol. In beer making, ale yeast ferments at the top of the liquid and prefers temperatures of about 60 degrees Fahrenheit to work its magic. Ale yeast produces a complex, fruity, sweet flavor in the beer. Ales are said to be "top fermented."

Lager yeast ferments at the bottom of the liquid and at much colder temperatures—down to 33 degrees Fahrenheit. Lager yeast was first used in brewing in the 1400s, though not isolated until the mid-1800s. Lagers are soft, rounded, less complex, dry, and refreshing. Lager beers are said to be "bottom fermented."

Yeast contributes subtly to almost every characteristic of beer, including dryness, sweetness, and mouth feel. Truly unique beers are that way because of their yeast, which may have been propagated continuously, in some cases, for several centuries.

When yeast is added to the beer before bottling it will leave a small cake on the bottom of the bottle. This beer is called "bottle conditioned." Yeast is a delicious—if cloudy—addition to the beer, and it's packed with vitamins and minerals.

When the ancient Egyptians worshiped the goddesses of beer they really were honoring a living creature without whom beer would not be possible. That critter was a fungus that we call yeast. Invisible to the naked eye, and virtually unknown and unnamed until the eighteenth century, yeast is what turns barley soup into beer.

Of course, those little yeasts floating around the atmosphere are also responsible for bread, wine, cheese, tofu, yogurt, and dozens of other foods we take for granted. But it is through their yeasty persistence at survival that all beer is made possible—from pilsner to porter.

Wild yeasts are everywhere, as anyone who has left unpasteurized apple juice out too long will attest to when they end up with hard cider. Yeasts thrive in the skins of fruit and are in wild abundance on the skins of grapes. In that way, wine is as natural as a tree or flower.

Until relatively recently, brewers and wine makers were basically ignorant of the invisible fungi around them—and who can blame them. While wine makers had the natural yeast advantage, brewers depended on airborne yeasts to turn water into beer. But this method had an inherent problem—some yeasts don't taste very good. In fact, all living things eventually rot because of yeasts. Those fungi are not welcome in the brewhouse.

In the old days of wooden brewing tubs and barrels, favorable yeasts took up residence in the porous wood. So too in the stirring sticks and spoons. Long before science isolated brewer's yeast, provincial home-brewers thought their vessels were blessed with brew voodoo. They handed these tools and amulets down from generation to generation. Spirits, prayers, and mystical mumbo jumbo were chanted and credited for (barley) water turning into beer. Today the only commercially produced beers utilizing wild yeasts are lambics from Belgium.

Yeast is the main thing that gives the same style beer from two different breweries two different flavors. A yeast strain that has lived in a brewery for hundreds of years will be as unique and individual as a fingerprint.

Many breweries have had disaster strike, and, for no apparent reason, their yeast turns into an enemy. Beer becomes soapy, vinegary, and just plain bad. Thousands of gallons of beer are consequently dumped down the sewer. In America, the brewer must contact the Bureau of Alcohol, Tobacco, and Firearms before dumping the bad beer to prevent being taxed for its production. Calls must also be made to local sewer departments to warn them that a living, toxic substance is headed for their processing station. All in all, the unhappiest day at the brewery.

Today's brewers protect themselves by keeping a pure strain of their yeast hidden in the brewery for emergencies. Others keep them off-site. Germany, Copenhagen, and England have yeast "banks," where breweries can safely store their yeast in case disaster strikes.

ALE YEAST   The earliest brewers realized that their wort was working when they saw the rocky, brown foam rising to the top of the tub. Through experience, they realized that if they saved some of that foam, they could use it to start another batch of beer.

Through natural selection, all ale and wheat beer brewers ended up using a strain of ale yeast, which was later named *Saccharomyces cerevisiae*. Ale yeast is not as efficient as lager yeast. Consequently, it leaves behind unfermented sugars that give ale its sweetness, fruitiness, butteriness, and complexity.

For centuries, ale was the only yeast available, and brewers worked through cool winter weather to make enough beer to enjoy throughout the summer. Once the air temperature got too warm, all sorts of unpleasant yeasts and mold would prevent beer making.

Yeast can be trained. In the old days, brewers made beer in open fermenters where the yeast could be gathered easily. In today's modern breweries, the yeast has learned to gather at the bottom of conical vessels. But this method causes the yeast to lose its ale characteristics, and so it must be repropagated after a few batches.

Ale is usually fermented for about one week. The yeast is removed, and the beer will have two weeks secondary fermentation. Sometimes another dose of yeast is added to the beer before bottling to give it natural carbon dioxide bubbles.

LAGER   In the middle ages, Bavarian brewers left their beer in mountain caves to protect it from the summer's heat. Through empirical evidence, the brewers deduced that this would protect the beer from contamination by wild yeasts. Unbeknownst to the brewers, the yeast in the beer also sank to the bottom of the barrel in the cold temps, where interbreeding with wild interlopers was not possible. The Germans called this *lagerund*, or storage.

Thus were yeasts trained to produce certain flavors in beer. When refrigeration was invented in the late 1800s, beer barrels came out of the caves and into the frigid tanks of the brewery. Until that time, breweries not located in mountainous regions had to hire laborers to dig miles of underground tunnels by hand so the beer could be lagarund.

People who remember their high school history might recall that Anton van Leeuwenhoek discovered the microscope in the eighteenth century. What they (probably) did not tell you is that Leeuwenhoek was looking at beer yeast the first time he used his new invention.

After studying yeast extensively, brewers began to understand that there were different strains that could provide different styles. By the 1800s, brewers in Bavaria were able to isolate lager yeast. A brewer at Calsberg Brewery in Copenhagen isolated a pure culture of lager yeast in 1883. To honor his discovery, lager yeast was named *Saccharomyces carlsbergensis*. The name was later changed to *Saccharomyces uvarum*.

Lager yeasts take longer to work but are more efficient. They consume more sugars in the beer, giving lagers a drier, cleaner, rounder, flavor—though less complex. Some say real lagers have the smell of new-mown hay from their yeast.

Lager beer is fermented at 41 to 48 degrees Fahrenheit for ten days to two weeks. During a three-week secondary fermentation, the lager temperature is lowered to 33 degrees Fahrenheit. Good breweries mature their lager at near-freezing temps for four to six weeks. Some quality brews may go as long as three months to a year. Cheap mass-produced beer may be lagered for only two weeks.

When a dose of yeast is added to lager before bottling, this secondary fermentation is called *kräusening*.

The Wheel of Flavor: Flavors Found in Beer, From Roses to Burnt Rubber

Have you ever had a beer that tasted grassy? How about leathery? Soapy? Well, you're obviously not a home brewer. Mistakes made in home brewing can bring out flavors that would make Beelzebub proud. That aside, beer experts can determine something like 120 different flavors in beer. Experts do things like sniff cardboard that has been marinated in beer for a week to recognize that smell as it reveals itself in poorly handled beer.

Many of those 120 flavors and smells are not desirable in a beer. But beer is complex, and it is possible to taste and sniff dozens of pleasing properties in a good beer. It's also good to know what the possibilities are when you're trying to write down your impressions of a beer. Sometimes it gets a little confusing because a slight butterscotch flavor in a Scottish ale is desirable. But in a lager the same flavor shows signs of poor quality. And some beers, notably Belgian Trappist-brewed Orval, can have a leathery taste and still be delicious.

Here is a shortened list of some of the types of flavors you might detect in a great beer.

alcohol	nutty (almond)
clove	butter
winey	butterscotch
fruity (apple, currant, berry)	hoppy
floral (rose)	malty
sherry	caramel

molassass
licorice
yeasty
leathery
sweet
honey
vanilla
tart
bitter

burnt
smoky
roasted
crackers
toast
grassy
strawlike
coffee

Just for fun, here's some awful types of flavors that are recognizable in beer. Home brewers might be familiar with these, but if you taste any of them in the beers listed in this book, take the stuff back to the store from whence it came.

plastic (bandages)
solventlike (acetone)
corny (chickenfeed)
tar
cheese
soap
fat
goatlike
catty
rancid
kerosene
machine oil
sulfur
rotten eggs

garlic
burnt rubber
shrimp
cooked cabbage
onion
wet cardboard
mold
must
salt
rust
metallic
puckery
powdery

I hope you'll be tasting a lot of the good flavors and none of the bad flavors. Although I'd say beers containing the latter outnumber beers with the former. Usually the larger the brewery and the cheaper the beer, the more you're likely to tread in the waters of catty, wet-cardboard beer.

Appendix C

Beer Festivals and Events

If you want to taste a lot of beer in a very short time, my advice is get thee to some beer festivals. There you will be given small glasses of dozens of beers. I like to take along my little pocket cassette recorder so I can keep track of my beer impressions. But hey, that's my job. Some folks just put on a raincoat and rubber boots and wade off into the sea of beer. By the end of the night, you'll have bumperstickers, buttons, glasses, T-shirts, and all the other breweriana paraphernalia that beer promoters can think of. And I hope it won't all be stuck to your face and hair.

Here's a list of some beer festivals that I found on the World Wide Web. If you want to do your own research and get exact dates and info, go to the Real Beer Page on the Web. Its address is http://realbeer.com.

Note: The dates of these events change from year to year, but I listed them in chronological order, as opposed to alphabetical by state. Good luck!

BEER FESTIVALS LISTED BY MONTH

February

> Northwest Microbrew Expo.
> Eugene, OR
> Lane County Convention Center
> America's Largest Winter Microbrew Festival
> Contact phone: 541-485-3907

> Shallo's Antique Pub Beer Tasting
> Indianapolis, IN
> Contact organization: Shallo's Antique Pub
> Contact name: Amy Shallobarger
> Contact phone: 317-882-7997

184

Toronado Annual Barley Wine Festival
San Francisco, CA
30 Barleywines on draft. Cigar smokers welcome.
Contact phone: 415-863-2276

Great Alaskan Winter Brew and Barley Wine Festival
Anchorage, AK
Held during Anchorage's Sixty-first Annual Fur Rendezvous Celebration
Contact phone: 907-276-BEER (2337)

Big Bear Brew-Ski—Winterbrew Fest
Big Bear, CA
Contact phone: 714-650-LIVE

Chocolate and Stout Festival
Dublin, CA
Contact phone: 510-829-9133

Kona International Brewers' Festival
Kailua-Kona, HI
Contact name: Spoon Khalsa
Contact phone: 808-334-1133

Febfest
Lake Bluff, IL
Contact organization: BOB (Brewers on the Bluff) and AHA registered
    homebrew club
Contact name: Steve Howard
Contact phone: 847-234-4150

Rogue Valley Micro Fest
Medford, OR
Contact phone: 206-303-0420

Charlie Papazian Gourmet Beer Dinner
Jericho, NY
Long Island Brewing Company
Contact name: Dave Glicker
Contact phone: 800-669-BREW

March

Classic City Brew-Fest
Athens, GA
Northeast Georgia AIDS Coalition

Admission: $18 in advance, $20 at the door
Contact organization: Brewtopia
Contact phone: (800) 540-MALT

Latvian Beer Tasting and Festival
Washington, DC
Contact phone: 202-293-1885.

Karnival of Beers
Fullerton, CA
Contact organization: Fullerton Hofbrau
Contact phone: 714-870-7400

Annual International Beer Festival
Peoria, IL
Contact organization: The Peoria Jaycees and Specialty Import
    Distributing Co.
Contact name: Stephen King
Contact phone: 309-682-2500

Beermaker's Dinner: New York vs. the World
New York, NY
Contact phone: 212-322-7600/reservations

Texas Brewers Festival
Dallas, TX
Contact name: Larry Warshaw
Contact phone: 512-462-1855

Annual Southeastern Microbrewers Invitational Beer Festival
Durham, NC
Contact organization: Southeastern Microbrewers' Association
Contact name: Tyrone Irby
Contact phone: 919-490-1474

Annual Great Arizona Beer Festival
Phoenix, AZ
Contact organization: Sun Sounds
Contact name: John M. Forbes
Contact phone: 602-780-3523 or 602-231-0500
Contact E-Mail: forbes@primenet.com
Annual Berkshire County Brewers' Festival
Pittsfield, MA
Contact organization: LIVE 105.5 FM, The Brewery and The Berkshire
    Hilton Inn

Contact name: Stephanie King/LIVE 105.5 FM
Contact phone: 413-499-3333
Contact E-Mail: steph@live105wbec.com

April

Noordelijk Bierfestival
Groningen, the Netherlands
Contact phone: nl050 5420267
Contact E-Mail: derks@ivg.com

Annual Mid South Brewers' Festival
Fort Smith, AR
Contact phone: 501-782-9898

Eugene Microbrew Springfest
Eugene, OR
Contact phone: 541-344-2247

Texas Brewers' Festival
Houston, TX
Contact name: Larry Warshaw
Contact phone: 512-462-1855

Brewtopia
Calgary, Alberta, Canada
Contact organization: Alberta Theatre Projects and CAMRA Calgary
Contact name: Jack Penfold, president, CAMRA
Contact phone: 403-239-3907
Contact E-Mail: jpenfold@mtroyal.ab.ca

Annual Spring Beer Fest
Portland, OR
Contact organization: Rosewood Productions, Inc.
Contact name: Steve Woolard
Contact phone: 503-246-4503
Contact E-Mail: springfest@jhw.com

Beer Tasting and Chili Cookoff and Blue Grass Jam
Lakeport, CA
Lake County Fairgrounds
Contact phone: 707-263-5092

The Annual Beerfest
Santa Rosa, CA
Contact phone: 707-887-7031

May

Annual California Festival of Beers
San Luis Obispo, CA
Join beer connoisseurs and select from over 65 California breweries, pro-
    ceeds benefit Hospice of San Luis Obispo County, a nonprofit organi-
    zation providing quality care to the terminally ill
Admission: $32, $5 for designated drivers
Contact organization: Hospice of San Luis Obispo County
Contact name: Marcy Villa
Contact phone: 805-544-2266 or 800-549-1538

Okanagan Fest of Ale
Penticton, British Columbia, Canada
Penticton Trade and Convention Center
Contact phone: 604-492-0852

Brew Erie
Erie, PA
Contact organization: Bert's Eastside Beer
Contact name: Ray Carr
Contact phone: 814-455-9083

Brew Ha Ha
Half Moon Bay, CA
Contact organization: Coastside Infant/Toddler Center
Contact name: Jill Anderson
Contact phone: 415-726-7416

Annual Yeast Feast
Williamsport, PA
Contact organization: Smed's Breads
Contact name: Bill Smedley
Contact phone: 717-398-7383

Grainaissance Faire
Glen Ellen, CA
Contact phone: 707-939-9666

Fifth Annual Boston Brewers' Festival
Contact phone: 800-565-4BREW

Belle Grove Beer Festival
Middleton, VA
Contact phone: 540-869-2208

Annual Hilton Head International Beer Festival
Hilton Head Island, SC
Contact organization: Bear Foot Sports
Contact name: Mark Weisner
Contact phone: 800-689-3440

June

International Brewmasters' Festival
Vancouver, British Columbia, Canada
Contact phone: 604-732-3377

Celebrator Beer News Skunk Train Trip and Beer Tasting
Fort Bragg, CA
Contact phone: 510-670-0121

San Rafael Brewfest
San Rafael, CA
Contact organization: Pacific Tap and Grill
Contact phone: 415-457-9711

Great Eastern Micro Festival
Adamstown, PA
Contact phone: 215-484-4385

River City Real Beer Festival
Richmond, VA
15 Mid-Atlantic and Southeastern craft brewers, 40 beers in a street festi-
    val setting in downtown Richmond
Contact organization: East Coast Events/MASB
Contact name: "Barley Bob" Barker
Contact phone: 804-643-2826
Contact E-Mail: 76460.1104@compuserve.com

Idaho Beer Festival
Boise, ID
Contact phone: 208-342-6652

Hayward Blues and Brew Festival
Hayward, CA
Contact phone: Tickets: BASS 510-762-2277 Info: 510-537-4341

Tessenderlo, Belgium
Over 100 special Belgian beers
Contact organization: De Limburgse Neus vzw

Contact name: Rene Heselmans
Contact phone: + 32 13 66 10 87 (fax +32 13 66 70 42)
Contact E-Mail: theselmans@versaversa.be

Annual Great New Jersey Craft Beer Fest
Vernon, NJ
Contact organization: Ale Street News
Contact name: Tony Forder
Contact phone: 201-368-9100

Colorado Brewers' Festival
Fort Collins, CO
Contact phone: 800-274-FORT

Summer Fest
Roseville, CA
20 microbreweries
Contact organization: The Active 20-30 Club of Roseville, CA

Great Hawaiian Beer Festival/Competition
Honolulu, Anahola, Kula, Kona, HI
Hawaiian Public Radio Beer Tasting
Contact organization: Hawaiian Homebrewers' Association
Contact name: Anastasy Tynan
Contact phone: 808-259-6884
Contact E-Mail: brew@lava.net
Contact URL: http://www.lava.net/~brew

Annual California Brewmasters' Classic
San Francisco, CA
Contact phone: 408-375-7275

Annual Mountain Brewers' Beer Festival
Idaho Falls, ID
Contact organization: Colonial Arts Theater Restoration Project
Contact name: Bob E. Beckwith
Contact phone: 208-346-6870
Contact E-Mail: bfirth@srv.net

Great California Beer Fest
Los Angeles, CA
Contact organization: Even Fest Productions
Contact phone: 310-328-8448

Mondial De La Biere/Beer Mundial
Montreal, Quebec, Canada

Largest international beer event in North America
Contact organization: Mondial De La Biere
Contact name: Pierre Lalumière
Contact phone: 514-722-9640
Contact E-Mail: Marois@Login.Net

World Beer Cup
Vail, CO
Featuring 3,000 breweries from more than 100
     countries
Contact organization: Association of Brewers

Annual Wichita Festival of Beers
Wichita, KS
Contact name: Beverly Moore
Contact phone: 316-838-7707, ext. 1222

Heartland Brewfest III
Adel, IA
Contact organization: Old Depot Brewery

Summerfest
Roseville, CA
Placer County Fairgrounds
Contact phone: 916-261-1117

International Beer Festival
Burlington, VT
Craft breweries and imports represented by invitation only
Contact phone: 802-388-0727

July

Savannah Suds Beer Festival
Savannah, GA
Contact phone: 803-689-3440

KQED International Beer and Food Festival
San Francisco, CA
From the great microbreweries of the West Coast to exotic imports from
     20 nations, over 250 different brews, the world taste tour is America's
     largest international brew and food fest.
Contact organization: KQED
Contact phone: 415-553-2200

Small Brewers' Festival of California
Mountain View, CA
125 beers from over 40 of California's finest microbreweries
Contact phone: 800-965-BEER

Oregon Brewers' Festival
Portland, OR
America's largest brewfest
Contact organization: Oregon Brewers' Festival
Contact phone: 503-226-7623

August

Blues Brew Fest in the Park
Concord, CA
Contact phone: 510-825-7665

Tahoe Fat-Tire Micro Festival
Lake Tahoe, CA
Contact phone: 916-581-1800

Great Southern Brewers' Festival
Atlanta, GA
Contact phone: 617-547-2233

Denver Post LoDo Brewfest
Denver, CO
Contact phone: 303-458-6685

Beer and Sweat
Ft. Mitchell, KY
Contact name: Tim "TBird" Thomas
Contact phone: 606-291-4843
Contact E-mail: tbird@iglon.com

The Great Taste of the Midwest
Madison, WI
Contact organization: Madison Homebrewers' Association

HopFest
Pleasanton, CA
35 microbreweries
Contact organization: The Valley Volunteer Center
Contact names: Dan Mays, Linda Chew
Contact phone: 510-462-3570
Contact E-Mail: hopyard@aol.com

Great Rocky Mountain Beer Festival
Copper Mountain, CO
Contact phone: 303-968-2318

Antique Street Fair and BrewFest
Gilroy, CA

Brewstock
Tacoma, WA
Contact phone: 206-232-2982, ext. 15

Annual Boulder Festival
Boulder, CO
Contact phone: 303-444-8448

Southern Brewers' Festival
Chatanooga, TN
25 breweries from the Southeast
Contact organization: Southern Brewers Association
Contact name: Brooks Hamaker
Contact phone: 800-737-2311
Contact E-Mail: bhama@aol.com

Second Annual WMFE Beer Festival
Orlando, FL
Contact phone: 407-273-2300

CAMRA Campaign for Real Ale's Annual Real Ale Fest
London, England
Contact Name: Stephen Cox or Ian Loe
Contact phone: 01727-867201

International Beer Festival
San Jose, CA
Contact name: Kevin Lytle
Contact phone: 408-236-2258

Mount Snow Brewers' Fest
Mount Snow, VT
Contact phone: 802-464-3333

September

Berkeley Beer Festival
Berkeley, CA
Contact phone: 510-THE-ROCK

Festibiere de Chambly
Chambly, Quebec, Canada
Contact phone: 514-658-1200

Oktoberfest
Fort Lauderdale, FL
Two consecutive weekends
Contact organization: City of Fort Lauderdale
Contact name: Marie Rock
Contact phone: 305-761-5360; fax 305-761-7135
Contact E-Mail: netwares@ix.netcom.com

Great Northwest Microbrewery Invitational
Seattle, WA
Over 100 different beers are represented
Contact organization: Festivals Inc.
Contact name: Dennis Masel
Contact phone: 206-232-2982

Great Lakes Extravaganza
Traverse City, MI
Contact phone: 616-938-3247

Charleston International Beer Festival
Charleston, SC
Contact phone: 803-689-3440

Micro Brew and Blues Festival
Fairfield, CA
Contact phone: 707-422-0103

Annual Brewfest
Irvine, CA
Contact phone: 310-926-2000

New York BeerFest
New York, NY
The Fund for the Borough of Brooklyn, Inc.
Contact name: Martha Bear Dallis
Contact Phone: 718-855-7882

Mid-Atlantic Beer and Food Festival
Washington, DC
Contact phone: 703-527-1441

MS After Dark
Providence, RI
Contact organization: RI Chapter of National Multiple Sclerosis
    Society
Contact name: John Messier
Contact phone: 401-723-9980

Great Eastern Micro Festival—Stoudts Festival
Adamstown, PA
Contact phone: 717-484-4387

California Midstate Varietal Beer Festival
Atascadero, CA
Contact name: Charles Higel
Contact phone: 805-544-1503

Taste of Morgan Hill
Morgan Hill, CA
Contact organization: Morgan Hill Chamber of Commerce
Contact phone: 408-779-9444
Contact E-Mail: garrie@garlic.com

Annual Rhode Island International Beer Exposition
Providence, RI
Contact phone: 401-274-3234

Annual Steamboat Fall Foliage Festival and BrewFest
Steamboat Springs, CO
Contact organization: Steamboat Springs Chamber Resort Association
Contact phone: 970-879-0880
Contact E-Mail: skramer@steamboat-chamber.com
Contact URL: http://www.yampa.com/steamboat-chamber

Brew Fest—Santa Rosa Bay Brewery
Walton Beach, FL
Contact organization: Santa Rosa Bay Brewery and Cafe
Contact phone: 904-664-2739

Oldenberg Beer Camp
Fort Mitchell, KY
Oldenberg Brewery
Contact organization: Oldenberg Brewery
Contact phone: 606-341-7223

Great Truckee River Beer Festival
Reno, NV
Contact organization: American Heart Association
Contact E-Mail: kirk@reno-brewing.reno.nv.us
Contact URL: http://www.connectus.com:80/~aztech/renobrew/
    gtrb-festival.html

Colorado Springs Microbrewers' Exposition
Colorado Springs, CO
Contact phone: 719-632-0553

First Myrtle Beach Beer Festival
Little River, SC
Contact phone: 303-447-0816

Annual River City Real Beer Festival
Richmond, VA
Contact organization: MASB/Mid-Atlantic Association of Craft Brewers
Contact name: Bud Hensgen
Contact phone: 703-527-1441
Contact E-Mail: budh2erols.com

Great Northwest Microbrewery Invitational
Seattle, WA
Contact organization: Festivals Inc.
Contact name: Dennis Masel
Contact phone: 206-232-2982

October

Sippin by the River
Philadelphia, PA
Contact organization: Penn's Landing Corp and Patricia Goodwin
Contact name: Patricia Goodwin
Contact phone: 803-768-6764

The Great American Beer Festival and The Virtual GABF
Denver, CO
1,350 different beers from more than 300 breweries

Annual Newport Brews and Blues Festival
Newport, OR
Contact organization: Lincoln Company Food Share
Contact name: Michelle Glenn
Contact phone: 503-265-4649

12th Annual Calistoga Beer and Sausage Fest and Chili Chaser
Calistoga, CA
Contact organization: Calistoga Chamber of Commerce
Contact name: Shirley Lauborough
Contact phone: 707-942-6333
Contact E-Mail: ca94515@aol.com

Quivey's Grove Annual Beer Fest
Madison, WI
Contact phone: 608-273-4900

Annual Microbrewers' Octoberfest
Chicago, IL
Contact phone: 312-836-4338

Pint Bockbeer Festival
Amsterdam, the Netherlands
Contact organization: Promotion Information Traditional Beer
Contact name: Peter van der Els
Contact phone: 02520-22909
Contact E-Mail: petere@elmer.gor.eur.compaq.com

Real Ale Fest
Chicago, IL
Contact phone: 414-545-9246

Ft. Lauderdale Oktoberfest
Ft. Lauderdale, FL
Contact name: Ken Cameron
Contact E-mail: netwares@ix.netcom.com

Annual Home Brew U Conference and Beer Dinner
Seattle, WA
Contact phone: 206-622-1880

Great San Francisco Micro-Brew Ha Ha
San Francisco, CA
Contact phone: 415-627-6939

BrewFest
Birmingham, AL
Contact organization: Birmingham BrewFest
Contact name: Greg Hall or Marsha Drennan
Contact phone: 813-595-1269; 205-323-0569, respectively

Charleston International Beer Festival
Charleston, SC
Contact phone: 803-689-3440

Hilton Head Island International Beer Festival
Hilton Head, SC
Contact phone: 803-689-3440

San Jose Flea Market Octoberfest and Lumberjack Contest
San Jose, CA
Contact phone: 408-453-1110

Pacific Coast Brewfest
Santa Barbara, CA
Contact phone: 310-207-6904

Brabantse Bieren Festival
The Netherlands
Contact name: Promotion and Information Traditional Beer
Contact phone: +31 161 453721
Contact E-Mail: etmtvop@etm.ericsson.se

Great Canadian Beer Festival
Victoria, BC
Contact organization: CAMRA Victoria
Contact name: John Rowling
Contact phone: 604-595-7729
Contact E-Mail: jrowling@galaxy.gov.bc.ca
Contact URL: http://www.islandnet.com/BlaneysTravel/beerfest.html/

November

The Great Louisiana BeerFest
Covington, LA
Contact phone: 504-871-9400
Contact E-Mail: dosequis@neosoft.com
Contact URL: http://www.neosoft.com/~dosequis/glbf.html

The Taste of the Great Lakes
Frankenmuth, MI
Contact organization: Bibere, Inc.
Contact name: Jeff Hervert
Contact phone: 517-652-9081

Annual Maine Brewers' Festival
Portland, ME
Contact phone: 207-780-8229

Real Ale Rendevous
Philadelphia, PA
Contact organization: Beer Philadelphia
Contact name: Jim Anderson and Chris Morris
Contact phone: 215-568-5603

American Red Cross Annual Auction, Microbrew and Wine Tasting
Denver, CO
Contact phone: 800-447-4886

Den Stora Idrickar Dagen
Sweden
Drink as much as U want of the Swedish beer
Contact organization: Juridiska Freningen
Contact name: Mikael Svegfors
Contact phone: +46-46393898 or +46-707303002
Contact URL: http://www.ts.umu.se/~jan/bilder/ford17m.jpg

Brew-Ha-Ha/Texas Brewers' Festival
Austin, Texas
Contact organization: Texas Brewers' Festival

Great Belgian Beer Festival
Belgium
Contact name: Peter Crombecq
Contact phone: + 32 16 651093 (tel. and fax)
Contact E-Mail: PCrombecq@AntwerpCity.be
Contact URL: http://www.dma.be/p/bier/7__2__uk.htm

Annual Paumanok Craft Brewers' Festival
Long Island, NY
Contact Phone: 516-932-1091

Annual Rhode Island International Beer Expo
Providence, RI
Contact organization: Festivals of America, Ltd.
Contact name: Maury Ryan
Contact phone: 401-272-0980
Contact E-Mail: RICider@aol.com

APPENDIX D

The Agony of De-Wheat: Beers That Didn't Rank in the Top Fifty

There are hundreds of great beers out there and more so-so ones. I hope I mentioned some of your favorites. Space, however, doesn't allow me to list all beers that were contenders for this book but for some reason didn't make it. Here are beers that nearly made the fifty best list and aren't mentioned under "Recommended Related Beers" in the text.

Abita Turbodog—Great name, great beer from the shores of Lake Pontchartrain down Loo-See-Anna way.

Anchor Steam/Porter—Great beers from the Bay Area.

Ballard Bitter Pale Ale—A great pale ale from Redhook.

Bateman XXXB Ale—A wonderful triple-X English stout.

Beavertail Dark Ale—A great, heather-scented Canadian ale that is closer to an India Pale Ale than a dark ale.

Big Shoulders Porter—One of the world's better porters from a great Chicago brewery.

Blue Moon Nut Brown Ale—A new offering by Coors trying to cash in on the micro market, brewed by F. X. Matt. A good nut brown.

Boon Faro Pertotale—A strong, sweetened lambic from Belgium.

Boon Gueuze—probably the most sour beer on the planet—yum!

Boon Kriek—An extremely sour Belgian fruit lambic.

Boulder Porter—A workmanlike porter for everyday drinking.

Brakspear Henleys Ale—A great English ale.

Granville Island Bock—A Canadian bock.

Grimbergen Double Ale—A Belgian offering.

Hoegaarden—A lovely Belgian wheat beer.

Kostritzer Schwarzbier—Literally "black beer" from Kostritzer, a formerly East German brewery.

Mackeson XXX Stout—One of the best sweet stouts around.

Our Special Ale—A great holiday offering from Anchor Steam Brewery in San Francisco.

Pike Place Stout—A stout for everyday drinking made by the brewery owned by the folks who are Merchant du Vin, one of the country's premier importers.

Pyramid Wheaten—The first wheat beer to be brewed in America since Prohibition ended—Pyramid revived the style that hundreds of microbreweries have since copied.

Rogue Smoke Ale—Like the rest of the Rogues, a great ale.

Samuel Smith's Lager—The best English lager.

St. Georgen Braü Keller Bier—A gold-medal-winning beer from Germany.

Schierlinger Roggen—A fantastic German rye beer.

Thomas Hardy's Country Bitter—A bitter ale from the folks who bring you the rare and expensive Thomas Hardy's Old Ale.

Thomas Kemper Hefeweizen—An American microbrewed product from the Hart Brewing Company, makers of Pyramid Ales. Kemper Hefeweizen is a stunning example of a cool, refreshing Berliner weisse, straight from the West Coast.

Watney's Cream Stout—About the only imported cream stout to be found in America, although lacking lactose, still a great beer.

Weihenstephan—Great beer from one of the world's oldest German breweries.

Yuengling Porter—A dark beer from America's oldest brewery.

APPENDIX E

Terms of Enbeerment: A Glossary of Beer and Brewing Terms

ale   The style of beer made with ale yeast, which ferments at the top of the wort. Ales are generally not aged as long as their cousins, lager beers. Ales are expressive, fruity, and complex in flavor.

altbier   Literally, "old beer" in German, the style that preceded lager. Altbier is a copper-colored German ale, usually associated with the city of Düsseldorf.

barley   The main ingredient in beer, sprouted barley is kilned at high temperatures to turn it into malt.

barley wine   A very strong ale, 8 to 10 percent alcohol by volume.

barrel   A term used to measure brewery output, one barrel equals 31 U.S. gallons of beer.

beer   A fermented drink made mainly from malted grain and usually seasoned with hops. In German, *bier*.

belgian lace   The lovely pattern that a great beer head leaves on the side of the glass as the beer is drunk. Belgian beers are famous for their creamy, rich foam and Belgium is famous for its lace.

bitter   A British style ale with a high hop content, making it, well . . . bitter.

bock   A strong, usually dark German lager, usually served in spring.

bottle conditioned   A beer that has yeast added to it right before bottling. The yeast causes the beer to referment and carbonation to develop naturally in the bottle. This is also known as *méthode champenoise*, the method used in making champagne.

bottom fermented   A beer made with lager yeast, which ferments at the bottom of the beer tun, lessening the chance of contamination and leaving a clearer beer.

brewery   A place where beer is made, generally in quantities exceeding 25,000 barrels a year.

breweriana   Brewing memorabilia such as old beer cans, trays, and advertisements.

brewpub   A tavern or restaurant that also makes its own beer, usually, but not always, for sale only on premise.

brown ale   A mild brown beer associated with Great Britain, where it is brewed to varying degrees of sweetness.

cream ale   An American-style beer that is mild, sweet, and golden in color. Some are brewed with ale *and* lager yeast, with the ale fermenting at top and the lager fermenting at bottom, hence the term *cream*.

dark beer   A general term for, you guessed it, dark-colored brown beer.

doppelbock   Literally, "double-bock" in German. An extrastrong version of bock. In Germany, the names of all doppelbocks end with the suffix *-ator*, as in Kulminator (brewed by E.K.U.) and Animator (brewed by Hacker-Pschorr). Not for the faint of palate.

dunkel   Literally, "dark" in German. Dunkles are (what else?) dark beers.

export   In Germany, export is a drier and less hoppy lager than most pilsners. Everywhere else, the term means *premium*, which usually means nothing.

framboise   A Belgian-style lambic beer with lots of raspberries added.

fruit beer   Any style beer that has fruit added to it.

helles   Literally, "pale" in German.

hops   The cone-shaped flower of the female hop plant, used to flavor and bitter beer. Originally used as a preservative.

imperial stout   A very strong stout, 7 to 10 percent alcohol, originally brewed in Britain between 1780 and 1918 as an export to St. Petersburg in tsarist Russia.

India pale ale   A strong, bitter beer originally brewed in Britain for export to soldiers in India. Made strong to survive the long boat trip.

kölsch   A light, delicate, golden ale associated with Cologne, Germany.

kraeusen   Literally, "crown" in German. The process of kraeusening beer involves adding unfermented wort to the finished beer so that it develops carbonation (head) in the bottle. This process is also called bottle conditioning, which is easier to pronounce.

kriek   A Belgian lambic beer with cherries added—elegant and delectable.

lager   A beer made with lager yeast, which is bottom fermenting. Lagers are supposed to be stored for long periods at cold temperatures, giving the beer a soft, clean taste.

lambic   A Belgian ale that is low in carbonation and usually fermented with wild yeasts that float into the brewery on the air in the fall season. The taste can almost resemble a fine sherry or cider.

light beer   That American curse to good taste, light beer is usually a lightly hopped, watered-down low-cal imitation of pilsner.

maibock   Literally, "May bock" in German, maibocks, pale and tasty, are brewed in fall and brought out in spring to celebrate that season of love and awakening.

malt   Grain, usually barley, that has been kilned to develop maltose sugars, those delicious molecules that yeast needs to make alcohol and CO_2.

malt liquor   Not malty or a liquor, an Americanism for cheap, sweet beer that is high in alcoholic content.

märzen   A medium-strong, malty beer usually associated with Oktoberfests and fall celebrations. *Märzen* literally means "March" in German, which is the month the beer is *made* for consumption the following fall.

mash tun   A copper or stainless steel cook pot used for making beer. *Tun* means "tub" in German.

microbrewery   A brewery that makes under 35,000 barrels of beer a year for sale off-premises.

mild   An English beer that is dark and highly-hopped, hence bitter, but mild in alcoholic content.

Munich/Münchener   Munich, Germany, produces dark, spicy lagers with an almost coffee palate. *Münchener* is a term used to describe that beer style.

Oktoberfest   Legend has it that in the old days of Germany, before refrigeration, March was the last month that beer could be made because the warmer temperatures that followed would bring out the wild yeasts and spoil any beer made later in the season. By October, the *märzenbier*, or "March beer," was ready to be drunk, and millions of thirsty Germans were ready to celebrate the fall harvest with some freshly decanted brew. Today's version of Germany's Oktoberfest was started in 1810 to celebrate the marriage of the crown prince of Bavaria. The festival begins in late September and lasts sixteen days, ending on the first Sunday in October. Millions of people attend the annual festival in Germany, where some beer halls hold several thousand people. Mini-Oktoberfests are celebrated in many parts of the world. Many of the brewpubs in this book celebrate Oktoberfest.

old ale   Not ale that has been left in the back of your fridge too long, but a British term for a medium-strong dark ale usually consumed in winter. Old ales can be aged for several years.

pale ale   A fruity, milder version of the English-style India Pale Ale.

pilsener/pilsner/pils   The most imitated beer style in the world, pilsner was the first commercially made lager beer. First perfected by Czech brewmaster Frantisek Poupe in the town of Pilsen, Czechoslovakia (then Bohemia), Pilsner Urquell beer was produced in 1842 to the accolades of all. "Pils" is pale in color, has a beautiful hop bouquet, and is almost as bubbly as champagne. Almost all beer produced by the U.S. brewing giants is an Americanized pilsner that is less hoppy and not aged as long.

porter   An English style that was first brewed in London in 1730, porter can be very bitter and very dark, almost black. It was originally brewed for hard workers like porters and carters who needed a bracing, nourishing brew.

rauchbier   A smoky-flavored lager made around Bamburg and Franconia, Germany, produced with malt that has been wood smoked. Another, more dramatic, way to make rauchbier is to heat rocks over a wood fire until they are white-hot, then plunge them into the boiling wort. A Scottish-style smoked beer is made with malt that is kilned over burning peat. Some American microbrews sell peat-malted beer.

Reinheitsgebot   The German beer purity law that states that beer shall be made only with barley, hops, yeast, and water, with the exception of wheat beer, which has malted yeast added to it.

saison   A mildly sour summer ale produced in Belgium and flavored with spices or herbs.

Scotch ale   A malty, almost black, strong ale produced in Scotland.

gravity   The weight of a liquid when compared to an equal amount of pure water. This type of measurement is used to determine how much malt is in a beer, and hence, its alcoholic strength. If a beer has a specific gravity of 1.040, it is 1.04 times heavier than water.

steam beer   Steam beer is a uniquely American product first produced in California during the Gold Rush. It is produced using bottom-fermenting lager yeast at top-fermenting temperatures. Fermentation is carried out in long, shallow pans called clarifiers. At one time, twenty-seven breweries made steam beer in the San Francisco area. Today, it is made exclusively by Anchor Steam Brewing Company, which has registered the name as a trademark.

stout   Stouts are very dark, very heavy ales that are sometimes sweetened with sugar. In Ireland, Guinness—who invented the style—makes the most famous stout in the world. There are dry stouts and sweet stouts. Stouts are highly hopped.

top fermented   Beer made with ale yeast, which works at the top of the liquid and falls to the bottom when done.

Trappist ale   Strong, fruity ales made by Trappist monks in Belgium. It is bottled like champagne and is considered to be some of the finest beer in the world.

ur/urquell   Literally, "original source of" in German, hence Pilsner Urquell is the original pilsner.

weisse/weissbier/weizenbier   Weisse means "wheat" in German and the term is used for wheat beers that are anywhere from twenty to sixty percent wheat. Weizenbier is a refreshing summer drink with a clovelike bouquet. It is often garnished with a slice of lemon in the glass.

wheat beer   See weisse.

wort   The sweet liquid that is produced by cooking, or "mashing," malted barley during the beer-making process. Beer is called wort before the yeast is added to it.

yeast   A single-celled fungus (sounds good doesn't it?) that turns sugar into alcohol and CO_2. Beer is made with either top-fermenting ale yeast (*Saccharomyces cerevisiae*), or bottom-fermenting lager yeast (*Saccharommyces uvarum*, formerly *Saccharommyces carlsbergensis*).

APPENDIX F

Beer Books, Magazines, and Web Pages

In the past few years there's been some great books written about beers. They're wonderful to own, but if money's tight, some books are available at the library, possibly with beer-soaked pages.

The Association of Brewers, Inc., is a Colorado-based nonprofit corporation dedicated to brewers of beer and all those interested in beer and the art of brewing. They publish several excellent magazines. They also publish dozens of books on subjects, ranging from cooking with beer to beer dictionaries to brewing science to yeast technology. Many of the books listed below can be found through the institute. They also sell T-shirts, breweriana, and home-brew equipment. They'll send you a free catalog.

Write to them: Association of Brewers, P.O. Box 1679, Boulder, CO 80306-1679.

BOOKS

Beer by Greg Smith. A history of civilization and suds. Avon Books, 1995.

Beer Here by Stuart A. Kallen. A plug for my other beer book, which is a complete guide to almost 600 American microbreweries and brewpubs. Citadel Press, 1995.

Beer Companion by Michael Jackson. Authoritative information of brews and breweries. Illustrated with over 200 photographs. Running Press, 1993.

The Beer Directory compiled by Heather Wood. This book is a directory of breweries, brewpubs, microbreweries, well-stocked pubs and restaurants, beer festivals and celebrations, beer-related retail stores, museums, organizations, and publications. And its worldwide, from Alaska to Asia to Africa to Belgium and back. Storey Publications, 1995.

The Beer Enthusiast's Guide by Gregg Smith. This book tells you how to taste and judge beers from around the world. Everything you wanted to know about beer but were afraid to ask. Storey Communications, Inc. 1994.

Great American Cookbook by Candy Schermerhorn. Cooking with Candy is easy. From the elegant to the downright sinful, Candy cooks 217 recipes with beer. It could change your life. Brewers Publications, 1993.

New World Guide to Beer by Michael Jackson. Beers of the world, with over 100 photos. Running Press, 1988, reprinted 1990.

The Historical Companion to House-Brewing by Clive La Pensée. A fascinating look at the history of beer. Recipes from the fifteenth to the nineteenth centuries. Montag Publications, 1990.

The New Complete Joy of Homebrewing by Charlie Papazian. The bible of home brewing. Many of today's brewmasters started brewing with Charlie's book, which is loaded with helpful knowledge and encouragement. Charlie coined the phrase, "Relax, don't worry, have a home brew." Avon Books, 1991.

The Secret Life of Beer by Alan Eames. This self-designated "Beer King" is a cultural anthropologist as well as a great writer and funny guy. Full of amazing facts. Storey Publications, 1995.

MAGAZINES AND BREWSPAPERS

Believe me, 'cause I know, keeping up with all the new beers introduced in the last few years is a full-time job. But there's help! Plenty of otherwise perfectly sane folks keep track of all this stuff for you so you can worry about other things—like how to pay for said beers. Most of these folks have been around for a while, and they're getting better all the time. What follows is an annotated list.

Ale Street News—A brewspaper about New York and surrounding areas, available for free in many brewpubs and bars. Subscriptions available: Tony Forder, P.O. Box 1125, Maywood, NJ 07607; 201-368-9101.

All About Beer—A nationally published magazine all about beer, with new products, brewery openings and closings, reviews, etcetera. Published six times a year. Chautauqua, Inc., 1627 Marion Avenue, No. 41, Durham, NC 27705.

American Brewer—A magazine geared toward those whose business is beer, but still plenty of amusing articles and info about brewing for the layperson. Published by Buffalo Bill Owens, whose twisted take on life gives it that extra edge. American Brewer, Box 510, Hayward, CA 94543-0510.

American Breweriana Journal—A publication dedicated to brewing memorabilia and paraphernalia with microbrewery updates thrown in for good measure. American Breweriana Association, Box 11157, Pueblo, CO 81001.

BarleyCorn—A brewspaper for the mid-Atlantic region. George Rivers, BarleyCorn, Box 2328, Falls Church, VA 22042.

BeeR: the magazine—Another one of Buffalo Bill's publications. On the masthead he lists his job title as "a god." But don't let that scare you—he's kidding (I think). This is a superb magazine, full of great graphics, interesting articles, and stuff many of us have never even imagined about beer. Bill's taken the beer magazine concept and pushed it into the twenty-first century. Contact Bill at Box 510, Hayward, CA 94543-0171; 800-731-BEER.

Brew Hawaii Say aloha to beer in the pineapple state. P.O. Box 852, Hauula, HI 96717; 808-259-6884. E-mail: brew@lava.net.

Celebrator Beer News—This one is free in most bars and liquor stores. Celebrator, Box 375, Hayward, CA 94543.

The Malt Advocate—A magazine dedicated to beer and malt whisky. 3416 Oak Hill Road, Emmaus, PA 18049; 610-967-1083.

Midwest Beer Notes—A brewspaper concentrating on beer news from around the Midwest. Free at many bars and liquor stores or by subscription. *Midwest Beer Notes*, 339 Sixth Avenue, Clayton, WI 54004.

New Brewer—A magazine published by the Institute of Brewing Studies
for the technical-and business-oriented brewer. *New Brewer*, Box
1679, Boulder, CO 80306-1679.

Northwest Beer Journal—A brewspaper of the Pacific Northwest available free in many bars and liquor stores or by subscription. Northwest Publishing Company, 2677 Fircrest Drive SE, Port Orchard,
WA 98366-5771.

Pint Post—12345 Lake City Way NE, No. 159, Seattle, WA 98125; 206-
527-7331.

Southern Draft Brew News—A brewspaper for the South. Free at many
bars and liquor stores or by subscription. *Southern Draft Brew News*,
120 Wood Gate Drive, Canton, GA 30115; 770-345-1512. E-mail:
brewnews@aol.com.

Southwest Brewing News—An amusing brewspaper, published in Austin,
all about brewpubs and brewing in Texas, New Mexico, Arizona,
and southern California, among other places. Available free at
many bars and liquor stores or by subscription. *Southwest Brewing
News*, 11405 Evening Star Drive, Austin, TX 78739.

Yankee Brew News—A brewspaper of New England. Lots of history and
fun facts along with reviews and information about breweries.
Available free in bars and liquor stores or by subscription. YBN, Box
8053, J.F.K. Station, Boston, MA 02114.

Zymurgy—A magazine about home brewing published by the American
Homebrewers Association. *Zymurgy*, besides being the last word in
the dictionary, means "the art and science of brewing." AHA, Box
1679, Boulder, CO 80306-1679.

BEER-RELATED WEB PAGES

The most comprehensive listing of beer-related Web pages can be found
under the Yahoo banner: http://akebono.stanford.edu/yahoo/Entertain-
ment/Drinks/Alcoholic Drinks/Beer. Another comprehensive page dedicated to beer is the Real Beer Pages: http://realbeer.com.

The Association of Brewers runs the Institute of Brewing Studies, the
American Hombrewers Association, the Great American Beer Festival,
and Brewers Publications. They know everything there is to know about

American brewing: http://www.aob.org.aob.
   Some other web pages:
Anderson Valley Brewing: http://www.avbc.com/avbc/home.html
Buffalo Bill's Brewing: http://and.com/bb/bb.html
Marin Brewing Co.: http://and.com/mbc/mbc.html
Peter Combecq's Benelux-beerguide: http://www.dma.be/p/bier/beer.html
Redhook Ale Brewery: http://www.halcyon.com/rh/rh.html
The Virtual Pub and Beer Emporium:
   http://lager.geo.brown.edu:8080/virtual-pub/
Virtual Brewery Adventure: http://portola.com/TR/VBA/index.html
Virtual Brewpub—*BeeR: the magazine*: http://www.ambrew.com/
The Cheap Beer Server—Dedicated to serving info that all those uppity
   beer sites don't talk about: http://jaka.nn.com~tinsel/beer/